"Far too many companies today us[e] of compliance as an excuse to pu[t out] annual reports, in which the true performance that investors and s[eek] to see is buried in a swamp of clic[hés]. Claire Bodanis has written an entertaining handbook on corporate reporting which offers golden rules of structure, clarity and brevity for writers of all kinds."

Martin Vander Weyer, Business Editor, The Spectator

"Treating the annual report just as a chore, a mandatory review of the past, is wasteful. It can and should also be the Company's manifesto for the future. This book is a masterclass for everyone involved, including the chair."

Dr Gerry Murphy, Chairman, Tate & Lyle and Burberry

"I wish annual reports were as well written as this book."

Sir John Kay, author, the Kay Review

BY THE SAME AUTHORS

Claire Bodanis
(as part of the Dark Angels Collective)
Keeping Mum, Unbound 2014
Established – Lessons from the World's Oldest Companies, Unbound 2018
On Writing, Unbound 2019

Mark Forsyth
The Etymologicon, Icon 2011
The Horologicon, Icon 2012
The Elements of Eloquence, Icon 2013
The Unknown Unknown, Icon 2014
A Christmas Cornucopia, Penguin 2016
A Short History of Drunkenness, Penguin 2017

Adrian Hornsby
The Chinese Dream, 010 Publishers, 2008
The Good Analyst, IFG, 2012

Claire Bodanis

2021 edition

Trust me, I'm listed.

Why the annual report matters, and how to do it well.

with contributions from

Heather Atchison

Mark Forsyth

Adrian Hornsby

Neil Roberts

Jay Sheth

Kerry Watson

foreword by
Sir Donald Brydon

Chartered Governance Institute UK & Ireland

First published 2020
Second edition published 2021

Published by
CGI Publishing Limited
Saffron House, 6–10 Kirby Street
London EC1N 8TS

© CGI Publishing Limited, 2021

All rights reserved. No part of this publication may be reproduced, stored in a retrieval system, or transmitted, in any form, or by any means, electronic, mechanical, photocopying, recording or otherwise, without prior permission, in writing, from the publisher.

Publisher's editor: Benedict O'Hagan
Cover and book design and layout by Falcon Windsor

British Cataloguing in Publication Data
A catalogue record for this book is available from the British Library.

ISBN 978-1-86072-832-7

As with all legislation, the provisions of the Companies Acts and related legislation are open to interpretation and must be assessed in the context of the particular circumstances at hand, the articles of association of the company in question, and any relevant shareholders' agreement or other pertinent ancillary agreements. While every effort has been made to ensure the accuracy of the content of this book, neither the author nor the publisher can accept any responsibility for any loss arising to anyone relying on the information contained herein.

For Rowan Adams

ABOUT THE AUTHOR

Claire Bodanis

Claire is one of the UK's leading authorities on corporate reporting, and the founder and director of Falcon Windsor, a specialist corporate communications and reporting agency.

Claire came to corporate reporting by way of four years at Cambridge, editing mediaeval texts and honing a love of language and a knack for translating incomprehensible jargon into modern, clear English – the perfect foundation for helping UK plc communicate well with words.

Having spent time at two of London's largest corporate reporting agencies, Claire founded Falcon Windsor in 2004 and now works with some of the UK's best-known companies to deliver thoughtful, creatively excellent and meticulously accurate corporate communications.

Claire is the co-author of three books with the Dark Angels Collective – the world's first collective novel, Keeping Mum, published in 2014; Established – Lessons from the World's Oldest Companies, published in 2018; and On Writing, to which she contributed a chapter on corporate reporting, published in 2019. She is an Associate Partner of Dark Angels, a global network of trainers and writers whose philosophy is that business writing should be more human.

For contributors' biographies, see page 246.

CONTENTS

	FOREWORD by Sir Donald Brydon CBE	v
	NOTE TO 2021 EDITION	vi
¶	PROLOGUE **Can I have that in writing?** by Mark Forsyth	vii
✱	INTRODUCTION **Do it well** by Claire Bodanis	1
(•)	**AN INVESTOR'S VIEW 1** From a large institutional investor (anonymous)	11
❝	CHAPTER 1 **Telling stories and ticking boxes** What reporting's all about PART I How did we get here, and who's it all for? PART II Getting your story straight by Adrian Hornsby	15
(•)	**A LAWYER'S VIEW** From **Will Chalk** and **Richard Preston**, Addleshaw Goddard	59

CHAPTER 2
In or out?
What else reporting's about (and may be about soon)
by Claire Bodanis
65

CASE STUDY — 86
The story of ESEF: Part 1 – how not to create reporting regulations

The story of ESEF: Part 2 – how, with the right purpose, technology can ride to the rescue

---

CASE STUDY — 96
Get involved and influence the future of reporting: a look inside the FRC's Future of Corporate Reporting Project and its outcomes with **Thomas Toomse-Smith**

CASE STUDY — 100
Auditors should be thinkers, not bean counters: a discussion of the Brydon Review with **Paul Lee**

AN INVESTOR'S VIEW 2 — 105
From **Sacha Sadan**, Legal & General Investment Management

AN AUDITOR'S VIEW — 109
From **Maria Kepa**, EY

CHAPTER 3
Fail to prepare, prepare to fail...
How to get the report done well, with minimum hassle and stress
by Kerry Watson
113

ADDENDUM — 135
How to tackle reporting when working remotely, by **Claire Bodanis**

SPOTLIGHT ON DUAL-LISTED COMPANIES — 151
BP plc

SPOTLIGHT ON LARGE PRIVATE COMPANIES — 155
Arup

	CHAPTER 4	161
	Respect your reader	
	How to make your report useful and engaging – through writing and design	
	by Heather Atchison	

	SPOTLIGHT ON SMALL CAP COMPANIES	183
	The Vitec Group plc	

	CHAPTER 5	191
	Them = Us	
	How to work well with your agency	
	by Claire Bodanis	

	AN INVESTOR'S VIEW 3	213
	From **Andy Griffiths**, The Investor Forum	

	AN INVESTOR'S VIEW 4	217
	From **Andrew Ninian**, The Investment Association	

	CHAPTER 6	221
	Sweat the asset	
	How to get the best return on investment – make the annual report story the foundation of your communications	
	by Neil Roberts	

USEFUL SOURCES	238
ACRONYMS AND ABBREVIATIONS	242
ACKNOWLEDGEMENTS	243
CONTRIBUTORS' BIOGRAPHIES	246
CHAPTER NOTES	248
INDEX	250

FOREWORD
Sir Donald Brydon CBE

I HAVE BEEN WRITING CONTRIBUTIONS TO ANNUAL REPORTS for a quarter of a century and I thought I knew most of what there is to know about the purpose and production of these documents. This cleverly composed book has shown me that I was wrong. There is a lot to learn.

The contributions here helpfully contextualise the annual report and lay bare many of its inner tensions. As the role of the company evolves to embrace responsibilities to a wider group of stakeholders than just shareholders, so it becomes more important that the purpose of the annual report is clear. All those who interact with a company are united in seeking the answer to two central questions. Is this company honestly managed? And, is it likely to be around in a few years' time? The annual report becomes a very important part of answering those questions but, as the book says, it must be part of a coherent communication strategy.

I must expand on one remark made by a lawyer in the book: 'the purpose of annual reports is to build trust in business'. To my mind, it is the directors, managers and employees of a company who have the responsibility for building trust by their behaviour. This behaviour is communicated through the annual report which thus becomes the opportunity to demonstrate that such trust is appropriately earned. The purpose of the annual report is, then, to give all its readers the opportunity to understand the company as a result of an accurate description, both static and dynamic, of its affairs.

This applies both to statutory financial disclosures and to the other information the directors deem necessary to publish for clear understanding. This includes explanations of risks and performance against other factors such as, for example, the impacts of climate change. Helpfully the book endorses the benefits of bespoke reporting rather than the adoption of over-standardisation and slavish adherence to some universally defined 'best practice'.

Claire Bodanis has brought together a number of lenses through which to view annual reports. In the wake of the Covid-19 crisis, it will matter even more that companies tell their story openly and honestly. Their language choices are now susceptible to analysis by artificial intelligence. There will be renewed interest in the nuances in descriptions of risks and the policies to mitigate or accept them. Clarity and consistency will be valued in times of considerable anxiety. It is a time for outstanding communication. *Trust me, I'm listed* will help all those about to put pen to paper or fingers to keyboards. ∎

Note to 2021 edition

Since *Trust me, I'm listed* was published in June 2020, the reporting landscape has continued to evolve. Two key regulatory changes have come into force, with significant practical consequences:

- Filing the annual report in a digital format (the European Single Electronic Format, or ESEF) which is having consequences for process and production, and
- The requirement for UK premium-listed companies to report against the recommendations of the Task Force on Climate-Related Financial Disclosures, which is having perhaps more far-reaching consequences given that it asks companies to quantify the likely effects of climate change on their business.

Related to the second point, the expectations of stakeholders, particularly investors, have rocketed in the last year with regards to what companies are doing about environmental, social and governance, or ESG issues. Calls for a consistent approach to ESG reporting have led to various collaborative efforts towards standardisation, with the IFRS Foundation's proposed International Sustainability Standards Board looking likely to prevail.

None of this has had much effect on the practical guidance which is the bulk of this book. But even so, the sections – principally Chapter 2 – where we discuss the context of reporting felt in need of an update. And, while updating those, we also checked all data references and updated those where more recent statistics were available.

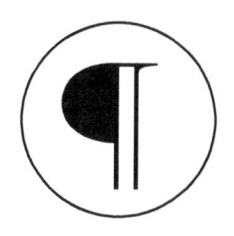

PROLOGUE

Can I have that in writing?

by Mark Forsyth

Can I have that in writing?

WRITING WAS INVENTED for corporate reporting. Everything else – all the sonnets, screenplays, novels, newspapers, histories, dictionaries, street signs, safety instructions, treatises, tracts, magazines, manifestos, pamphlets, biographies, bibles, booklets, leaflets, letters, articles, epics, e-mails and this book itself – everything else is a side effect. All the libraries and literatures of the worlds are nothing more than spin-offs.

That, at least, is how it would have appeared to the Mesopotamians of the late fourth millennium BC when they came up with their new system of scratching signs into wet clay. They wanted to do what we still want to do now: corporate reporting. They wanted to record and present financial plans and transactions, improve their corporate image, and generate trust in a complex society. Society, in Mesopotamia in the fourth millennium, had become terribly complicated. Society was too big.

You can only have 150 friends. You may have fewer, but it's very, very hard to have more. Put bluntly: your brain isn't big enough. This was worked out by an anthropologist called Robin Dunbar. He noticed that apes live in packs and that the apes with larger brains live in bigger packs. You can plot it on a graph of brain size against pack size and you get a nice neat correlation. That's because you need brain capacity (specifically neo-cortex capacity) to remember who's an alpha male, who's a beta, which female grooms whom and so on and so forth. Otherwise the pack would fall apart. The correlation between brain size and pack size is neat enough that you can extrapolate to see how big a pack of humans should be. The answer is 150.

Well, to be precise, the answer is 148; but the correlation isn't that neat, so 150 will do. Dunbar himself was pretty relaxed about it. He defined it as 'the number of people you would not feel embarrassed about joining uninvited for a drink if you happened to bump into them in a bar'. And his number didn't just depend on the apes. If you dig up a Stone Age settlement, which archaeologists are prone to do, you find that they never get much larger than housing and huts for 150 people. Once a village became larger than that, it seems, people would split off and go and found a new village in the next valley. That new one would grow, reach a population of 150, and the cycle would repeat.

That means that in a Stone Age settlement nobody ever needed to make notes. Everybody knew everybody. Therefore, if Zog the Hunter-Gatherer owed Zig 20 mammoth tusks everybody in the village knew of the debt, and if Zog didn't pay, everybody in the village knew that he was a dirty, rotten thief. Life is so simple when there are only 150 people about. There's no need for accounts or contracts, or annual reports. The human brain was enough. It was therefore something of a problem when, in the fourth millennium BC, the first cities were built.

A city is a complicated place, necessarily so. It doesn't produce its own food. So for city-dwellers to survive they have to pay farmers to bring them grain or whatnot from the countryside. To do that they have to have something to give the farmers, and somebody needs to keep track of who owes what to whom. You have to have such records when the size of a society has outstripped the size of the human brain. For civilisation to exist at all, you need accountants. That is why the first human whose name we know was an accountant.

The name is found on a set of accounts from the thirty-third century BC on a clay tablet not much larger than the palm of your hand. It's written in what's known as proto-writing. There are some symbols that show the accounting period (37 months). Then there's a symbol for barley (it looks like a stalk of barley). And then there are some symbols for units with numbers scratched beside them. We know what those units were, and it comes out at about 135,000 litres. And next to that the accountant has neatly signed his (or her) name: he (most likely – we are talking fourth millennium BC here) was called Kushim. No king, queen or emperor has had a name that has lasted so long.

This was still the time of proto-writing. There was no alphabet, just pictographic symbols, each denoting a particular thing. So Kushim signed his name using a rebus system. A rebus system is quite simple. It's when you use a series of pictures to punningly spell out a word. For example, the word 'carpet' could be a picture of a car followed by a picture of a pet. My surname – Forsyth – could be represented by the number 4 followed by a picture of a scythe.

In proto-writing there were only pictures of things. But the rebus system could string them together so that the pictures became an alphabet (or more precisely a syllabary). And with a syllabary, and a bit of ingenuity, you could write any Sumerian word. But originally, the rebus system was just what accountants used to sign their names.

Thus writing emerged. It was a game played by accountants to sign off their accounts. This early writing was of course slow to read, but in the end it *maid cents*. And that is how we know of long-dead Kushim. He was doing exactly what we are still doing now. Recording and presenting accounts so that in the complicated and confusing world of the Sumerian city state there was a clear and permanent record of what had happened, of who had paid what to whom, and of what goods had been supplied. It was corporate reporting.

But why did Kushim sign his name at all? He had no intention of making his name live forever, no idea that his would be the first name in history. Indeed, it wouldn't have been, had the clay tablet not been accidentally baked in a fire. (Generally Sumerian tablets were written in wet clay and that was it. Only those that, for some reason, were burned, survive to this today. It was the one time in history when a fire at a library was a good thing.) Kushim had to sign his name on his tablet in order to create trust, because business needs trust.

When we ask, today, 'Can I have that in writing?' it is because, essentially, we don't trust each other. We can't. There are too many of us. In the happy little Palaeolithic settlement of 150, everybody knew everybody else and could trust them (or knew not to). But in the Sumerian cities where thousands of people lived and traded, that had become impossible. Society had, five thousand years ago, grown too big for trust. In the modern world where business is done with billions, where even a single company can be much, much larger than an ancient city, we have to have things written down and signed.

Writing is a way of proving that something was said, and signing is a way of proving who said it. Even today, it is not enough that the accounts are done and audited. We need to know who did them, and who audited them. It's not enough to say something; you need to put it in writing and sign it off. This was then, and is still, the essence of a company's annual report. It sets in stone, or in clay, or on paper, what the company has achieved, what it is doing, and what it plans to do. It is not the opinion of a tipster, or a rumour doing the rounds. It is a signed and sealed statement that will rest unchanged while the world changes around it. It is also part of the brand.

The Sumerians loved branding too. They needed it as much then as we do today. The merchants and city states of Ancient Mesopotamia used cylinder seals. These were cylinders (as the name suggests) with pictures carved on them in reverse-relief. The result was that when you rolled them on wet clay a picture was produced, and, as you could keep rolling, the picture could, in theory, go on forever.

As ever, graphic design was important. The larger the city, or the richer the merchant, the greater the sophistication and beauty of the seal. This was, after all, the corporate brand. It was the sign that they, somebody who could be named and found, had put their logo on this product or that contract. When an image is going to define you, and define your trustworthiness, it's worth finding the best graphic designer for the job, somebody who understands what you stand for, how you want to be seen, and who can make you still look good when, in five thousand years' time, your logo is on display in the British Museum.

The world now is more complicated than it was in Kushim's time. Much more complicated. There are over seven and a half billion of us and (with a few exceptions) we can all do business with each other. We can do it by email, by instant money transfer, by blockchain or by algorithm. The food eaten in London can be (and often is) shipped from New Zealand. The human mind cannot hope to recall the tiniest fraction of our debts and dealings. That is why now, more than ever, we need the clear signed and sealed statement of a company's activities and accounts, and we need to have it in writing. ∎

INTRODUCTION

Do it well

by Claire Bodanis

THERE ARE TWO THINGS YOU OFTEN HEAR about reporting. One, it's really hard. Absolutely true. If you're new to reporting, it's important you know this now, so you can be prepared. And if you're an old hand, you'll know it as well as I do.

Two, it's a waste of time because no one reads the annual report anyway. Absolutely not true. I wouldn't have spent most of my career in this field if it were – nor would I have been asked to write a book about it, the research for which took me from company secretaries and governance professionals in companies large and small, to lawyers, auditors, investors, and to many who don't quite fit into any of those categories. The people I talked to overwhelmingly agreed that reporting, far from being moribund and unnecessary (and despite its many faults), is essential and, when done well, is central to both good business operations and corporate communications. It's at the heart of the relationship of trust between companies and their stakeholders. And it is that trust that enables companies ultimately to stay in business.

I use the word stakeholders quite deliberately here because reporting, although it grew out of the requirement to report to shareholders, has a much wider reach today. This is achieved not only through the annual report being read in its pure form, but through the many other ways the information it contains is used by a company, internally and externally. This gives the annual report an additional importance as the 'source of truth' about a business.

This idea of truth is something that I believe is more important than ever in today's world of fake news.[1] How do you determine fact from fiction? Whom do you trust? I believe corporate reporting has a fundamental role to play in the fight for truth. Yes, the report is a company's own view of itself. But, when done well – if it adheres to the spirit as well as the letter of reporting law, regulation and listing rules, and is audited thoroughly and objectively – I would argue it has the potential to be some of the most robust, accurate and honest of any information published today. And, therefore, to be of enormous benefit to both business and wider society.

So why do some people see reporting as a waste of time? It centres on those two words 'done well'. When reporting is done badly, this criticism is entirely fair. It's not necessarily that companies don't care – although it's true that some don't. Nor is it necessarily because some companies only pay lip service to the regulations by hiding behind reams of waffly, boring text – although it's true that some do. What is it then?

It comes back to the first point, that reporting is really hard to do well, and every year it becomes more so. The ever-ballooning regulatory requirements make it very difficult to produce something compliant, let alone coherent and engaging. And the increasing pressures to report more yet earlier mean that, as results day looms and the all-nighters get more frequent, 'as long as it's not wrong' becomes ever more appealing as the basis for a decision. So it's not surprising that the ambitions for doing it really well this year, with which the team set forth so hopefully a long six months ago, quite understandably go out the window.

Which brings me to why The Chartered Governance Institute asked me to write this book, and why I was so pleased to say yes. It's precisely because reporting is the most difficult, and yet the most important of corporate publications. And, until this book, there's been very little in the way of practical guidance for the doers[2] on how to do it well and how to make the doing a whole lot easier.

---

1 The Edelman Trust Barometer 2020 showed that 76% of respondents 'worry about information or fake news being used as a weapon', while 57% feel that the media they use 'are contaminated with untrustworthy information'. And, the Trust Barometer 2021 showed that overall, 50% of respondents thought that finding ways to combat fake news was more important than a year ago.

2 When I say the doers, I'm talking about the company secretaries and others who co-ordinate the whole process, and those who write and produce the strategic and governance reports. Finance teams are governed by IFRS, and generally have their process and production pretty much sewn up – and so this book does not include a technical guide to how to produce your financial statements. I hope, however, that finance teams will get something out of it anyway!

The first edition of this book was published in June 2020 when we were in the early stages of dealing with Covid-19; these made the practical challenges of reporting even greater. And so we included in the first edition a special section on the challenges of remote working and their impact on reporting at the end of Chapter 3. Now, more than a year later, remote working seems set to continue at least in some form. The challenges for reporting are no different, but we have the benefit of greater experience and so have updated that section accordingly.

Doing reporting well by understanding why
So what does this guidance look like? The philosophy of this book is that, if you understand why you're being asked to do something, you will do it much better than if you are simply told what to do. This is fundamental for reporting. While the principles behind what makes a report a good one are broadly the same for everyone, and the principles of getting it done are widely applicable too, what will make your report a good one is it being right for your company. And there is no single, right and only way of doing that – because the single, right and only way to do your report for your company is going to be unique to you.

It makes sense – after all, the regulatory perspective of reporting, in the UK at least, is principles-based not rules-based; it assumes rightly that every company is unique and has its own story to tell. Similarly, every company is a collection of different people who like to work in different ways, and has its own unique internal dynamic and its own processes. Of course there are regulatory boxes to be ticked, and you need to make sure that they are ticked, but the way that you do that should be unique to you. And, to come full circle, don't forget that one of those tick boxes is, in fact, to tell your own story.

What to expect in this book
What this book sets out to do is to explain, in six chapters, the principles behind reporting, drawing on the expertise of many skilled people across the reporting spectrum, who have kindly contributed their thoughts:
1. What the report is about, and how to make it into a story (the principles apply to the governance and remuneration reports as well, although the strategic report inevitably has more attention)
2. What else reporting's about (and may be about soon)

3. How to make what is a complex process as smooth and as easy as possible from planning to publication, including a special section on dealing with the challenges of remote working
4. How to make your report accessible and engaging through writing and design
5. How to work well with your agency
6. How to make the most of your annual report story as the foundation of your ongoing communications.

Each chapter has tips and takeaways, and we've designed this book in a way that, we hope, follows our own principles of being engaging and accessible.

Why we advise against best practice[1]
But what about best practice? Isn't there some kind of list? Well, there are lots of things out there that purport to be lists of 'reporting best practice', and tell you how to make your report 'best practice'. But in the context of this book, the answer's no: there is no list and you will not find the words 'best practice' used for anything in it, because there is no such thing as best practice. All those things out there, while they may be useful in some contexts, and indeed *good* practice, are not, and never can be, 'best practice'.

To do reporting well, your report has to be unique to you. The problem with labelling things 'best practice' – best practice risk reporting, for example, or best practice business model disclosure – is that it implies some kind of gold standard of what a report should look like or what it should say. For reporting there is no such standard – and nor do I believe there should be. There can of course be shared ideas and principles for useful ways of doing things, but a good report will always be a unique report.

---

[1] I was delighted to discover that mine is not a voice crying alone in the wilderness against the concept of best practice. Sir Donald Brydon, in his recent review into the quality and effectiveness of audit, uses even stronger language: 'I believe that this concept has been a pernicious addition to the lexicon and one that allows, indeed even encourages, lazy thinking. It is too seductive for people to retreat behind a best practice defence of their actions. What matters is that the right practice has been followed and that may well be different in different companies and at different times. What matters is what is right for a particular company, with its particular problems and its particular management at this particular moment given its particular circumstances. Best practice concepts drive out innovation as it is always safer to go with the herd and claim that an action is best practice rather than take a bolder and individual step.' *Assess, assure and inform: improving audit quality and effectiveness*, p.103.

From a practical point of view, labelling this or that 'best practice' does reporting a disservice, because it encourages people to copy what other companies do, rather than to think for themselves. I don't mean to imply that looking at what other companies do is a waste of time – of course it isn't. And there are conventions and ways of doing things that can be borrowed or shared to good effect – use of graphics, for example. But this borrowing and sharing only works if the ideas are properly adapted to what your company needs to communicate. The same is true for how to get the report done – as ever, there are useful principles to follow, but not some list of things that, if followed faithfully, will automatically result in the perfect report.

What makes a report truly 'best practice' (i.e. good) is whether or not it meets your company's objectives for reporting, and whether it tells your company's story in an engaging and meaningful way (while, of course, complying with all the regulations). What is 'best practice' for one company, therefore, may well not be for another.

And so, throughout this book, we encourage you to ask questions which will, we hope, help you find the right answer for your report, rather than shoehorning in the right answer from someone else's.

'Et al' as a reflection of reporting
I say 'we' because this book has been written by a group of us. My reason for mentioning them here is not to explain who they are (you can read their biogs on pages 246-247), nor to thank them for participating, important though those things are. Rather, in line with our theme, I wanted to comment briefly on why 'et al', aside from each person's skills and expertise, are such an essential part of the concept of this book.

An annual report is not a novel, the brainchild of a single author. Rather, it's a collective endeavour by what is often a very large group of people – (ideally) subject-matter experts, with different views and different writing styles. And, depending on the company, the person who ultimately holds the authorial pen will differ – if indeed, there is one person. When I was asked to write this book, my first thought was – who would be the best people to contribute? Reporting is a vast subject, and for this book to be truly useful, it needed more than I alone could give it. In fact, it needed the broad approach we take when writing an annual report. And what's that, exactly?

How to write a collective book

Writing a collective book isn't the same as writing an annual report – it's a lot simpler, for a start. But it poses the same challenge as any piece of writing that involves multiple authors: how do you get a consistent message, a coherent whole, when different people are writing different bits?

Either they must all write in the same tone and style and sound like one voice (in the case of an annual report, the company – more on that in Chapter 4), or they must be named, and speak in their own voices, but within the overall agreed message and story. The parallel of named voices with the annual report is, of course, the Board or senior executive statements, typically the Chair, CEO and CFO. What you want to avoid is difference where there should be consistency (the company voice), and blandness where there should be variety (named voices).

To bring it all together and create a coherent piece of writing from multiple authors, there are some high-level principles that apply just as well to annual reports as to this book, and which you'll see reflected in the advice in later chapters:

- A guiding brain that defines the overall story and writes some key chapters – me
- An editor to review everything and ensure consistency of message – also me
- A group of experts who know their material inside out – my co-authors
- A clear brief that sets out the story and plan, to which everyone contributes, and against which everyone writes their chapters – written by me, contributed to and agreed by all
- A firm hand managing a flexible schedule (it did run over Christmas, after all), that nonetheless has some fixed deadlines, including the publishing date – our project manager
- An approach to design that reflects the brief, namely that the book should be useful as well as a good read; it's not a novel, after all, so people need some visual help to encourage them to turn the pages – the creative team
- Absolute rigour and accuracy – thanks to our reviewers and proofreaders, although any errors are my own.

What you will find when reading this book, then, is a number of distinct authorial voices where chapters are written by my co-authors, akin to the distinct voices in the best executive statements. And running through them is a single, powerful message about the importance and value of reporting as the basis of the relationship of trust between company and stakeholder. This goes right back to the very origins of civilisation and the foundations of writing, as you'll have discovered in the (rather playful) prologue that precedes this introduction.

What I hope you'll also find is a real eagerness to share with you the principles of how to do reporting well, so that you can produce a report you can be proud of, and through a process that's a little less arduous. Given its complexities, reporting will never be easy. But thanks to the generous contributions of so many people to this book, and virtual working challenges notwithstanding, it could certainly become a whole lot easier. ■

A NOTE ON OUR RESEARCH FOR THIS BOOK

This book is a practical guide, so our research saw us interviewing as many people involved in reporting as we could – from companies large, medium and small, to investors of different types, to auditors, lawyers and other practitioners. We're very grateful for their insights which helped inform our views and improve our practical suggestions. Most have been anonymised – after all, people will speak far more candidly if we don't out them in print!

Instead of carrying out our own comprehensive surveys of investors, or of FTSE or AIM companies, we took quantitative data from some of the many useful surveys done by others, which we've referenced in the appropriate places. Our thanks to them as well.

What's lacking, unfortunately, is much input from the regulators, with the exception of some friendly folk at the Financial Reporting Council – soon (we hope) to be called the Audit, Reporting and Governance Authority (ARGA), who were kind enough to talk to us about their future of reporting project. Otherwise, we found getting people from the regulatory side to talk well-nigh impossible – and this speaks to one of the issues of reporting, namely that the ever-changing regulatory regime seems to have little understanding of the practical consequences for reporting of its recommendations. But more on that in Chapter 2.

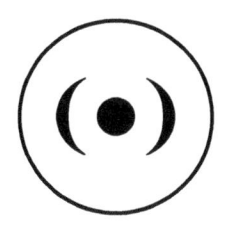

An investor's view 1

A conversation with one of the Middle East's largest institutional investors

Q – Is it true that large institutional investors don't read annual reports?
A – No way! The annual report is the first place I go when I think about taking a position in a company. It's a company's shop window for investors – our first handshake if you like, and it's where I start my due diligence. I look at the first few pages for the direction and strategy of the company, and if I get enough of a story, then I'll go to the financials. I'll spend a couple of hours with a report to begin with, then refer back to it for a few days as I do further research. If the story holds up, if it looks interesting, then I pick up the phone to the IR people. If the first few pages aren't clear, if they don't tell me a story, I shove it straight in the bin.

> **❝** *With so much money at stake I need written evidence of why I invested – and that's the annual report.* **❞**

Q – How about the results statement and presentation, or direct conversations with senior management – aren't they more useful?
A – They certainly have their place – I want to meet the management so I can judge them for myself (often against the annual report!), and the results give a good headline. But it's the annual report that gives you the full context that allows you to check whether the forward forecast of the results is accurate. Before I make any big investment in a company, I wait for the new annual report to come out. The other very important thing about the annual report is that it is all there in black and white – it's the proof of my investment. I can't give my investment committee a conversation with a CEO or CFO as an explanation for why I made a decision, particularly if things go wrong. With so much money at stake, the presentation or a conversation isn't enough. I need to be able to show written evidence of why I invested – and that's the annual report.

> **❝ *The annual report is an essential trust contract between the company and its investors.* ❞**

Q – How do you use annual reports?
A – Aside from the first introduction I mentioned, I use annual reports as reference documents throughout the year. This is especially important when something goes wrong – I'll go back to it and check whether there was a comment on the issue before I ring the company. If the issue wasn't mentioned, then it's a big problem, either because it calls into question the quality of the management – why didn't they see it coming? – or of their honesty – why was it missing? The annual report is an essential trust contract between the company and its investors, and if that trust is broken, it's very difficult to get it back. If I discover that a company has been wilfully misleading in its annual report, then I'll just get out.

Q – What makes a good annual report?
A – It's not about ticking the box. The story has to be clear enough for me to want to continue the conversation – so clarity of communications is essential. And it has to be consistent, and honest – not just for the initial investment, but for the continuation of the relationship, for the reasons I said about trust. Do not underestimate the negative power of an annual report done badly. It's a huge factor. If you mess up your annual report, an investor won't look at you. ■

CHAPTER 1

Telling stories and ticking boxes

What reporting's all about

by Adrian Hornsby

Questions this chapter will answer

Part 1: how did we get here, and who's it all for?
- What is the history of the annual report, and how does it help us understand the current form and future of reporting?
- Who reads reports, and how is their perspective different from the companies that write them?
- How can reporting make my company better?

Part 2: getting your story straight
- What is a story in the context of an annual report?
- How does this relate to the statutory requirements?
- How can I get better at telling my story, and make sure my readers understand it?

PART I

How did we get here, and who's it all for?

ONE WAY TO APPROACH THIS CHAPTER would be to set out a contents list for an annual report, and then work through it item by item, pasting in rules and regs and a lot of boilerplate guidance. I'd have fulfilled my chapter-writing obligations, and could spend the rest of the afternoon mixing cocktails. The only problem is I wouldn't have told you, the reader, anything you don't know already or can't find easily.[1] And this is fatal because, ultimately, you're the boss. You can stop reading any time, and as soon as you do, I've missed my moment.

When companies approach their annual reports with the question, 'What do I have to disclose?' they forget about their readers. Reporting obligations are fundamentally introverted concerns and, when used as the starting point, more often than not, produce reports that answer well to lists, but communicate little to people. Investors regularly complain about reports being too long, too pro forma, and too tick box-y – and for all that, not useful. Certain institutions may need to see that you've ticked your boxes, but what investors and others really want (and as they've said repeatedly throughout our research for this book) is to be *told a story*.

And so, to follow in the spirit of storytelling, rather than the letter of the list, I'm going to start by telling a story here – that of how the report became.

---

1 See useful sources, pages 238–241, or google 'annual report guidance'.

How the report became
As discussed in the prologue to this book, writing, cities, and even civilisation itself really got going with corporate records some 5,000 years ago. However corporate *reporting*, in its more modern sense of information that is prepared by a company, and reported to external shareholders, didn't start to take shape until the 1600s. The trigger was naval enterprise: in the newly globalised world, significant money was to be made by sailing across it and bringing back goods. Such ventures required capital, and so the captains of ships started selling stock in their seafaring trips. Initially investors came in on individual voyages, but as shipping entities scaled up and started to run multiple voyages concurrently, it became more convenient to invest in the shipping entity itself. Thus the modern company was born, together with its shareholders – and immediately with them, the demand for the company to tell them what it was doing with their money. Within a few short years this was taking the form of an annual financial one-pager. It looked a lot like a balance sheet.

1700s: the first bubble and its Act
The most significant of these early companies by far was the East India Company, which, thanks to its Royal Charter (effectively a monopoly on trade in the East), became fantastically rich and powerful. Its shareholders lived in mansions and lobbied the government. They also grumbled from the outset about the Company being secretive, and that the financial reports it provided were incomplete, but few thought that owning its shares wasn't still a very fine thing to do. A boom in commerce at the end of the seventeenth century led to a glut of new companies, and with them, share issuances, and because by then *shares themselves* had come to seem so wonderful, buyers in London coffee houses snaffled them all up.

By 1719, share enthusiasm was bubbling high. At this point, the South Sea Company – complete with a Royal Charter of its own – launched its much-anticipated public offering, and things tipped into frenzy. All manner of people were suddenly scrambling over each other to invest in the South Seas, in shipping, or indeed in anything else on offer, no matter how thin the information provided. At the height of the bubble's swell, one now-infamous venture described itself as: *'A company for carrying on an undertaking of great advantage, but nobody to know what it is.'* Its IPO raised £2,000 (equivalent today to millions) in the first six hours. Needless to say, this couldn't go on. The inevitable pop came in 1720 as companies both fake and real across a wide range of industries all collapsed, ruining thousands of people. Mass government corruption was revealed, and a freshly cleaned-out Parliament, desperate to be seen to be doing something, responded with the 'Bubble Act'. This declared that any company without a Royal Charter caught selling stock 'for ever be deemed illegal and void'.

1800s: the second bubble, and the beginnings of statutory reporting

This was a drastic measure, and Parliament eventually rolled back on it, but not for over a hundred years. When it did, the drive came again from new forms of enterprise. By the 1830s, the Industrial Revolution was taking hold, and technological advancement was creating whole new industries, such as railways, deep-pit mining and industrialised steel-making. These were all highly profitable, but again, capital intensive, and so once more the business case arose for raising investment by offering shares to the public. The government relented and created the necessary legal structures, but pretty quickly the same thing happened: in the 1840s 'railway mania' took hold, culminating in the 'railway scandal' of 1849. Companies collapsed, people went bankrupt in droves and, once again, there followed a regulatory backlash.

This time though, rather than banning shares outright, the focus turned to the information shareholders were being given. Investment was too powerful a tool to get rid of altogether, but if companies could be persuaded to be less secretive, so the thinking went, and simply 'tell it like it is', then shareholders wouldn't get so fooled, and then so burned, and the government could stay well out of it. An accounting requirement was passed into law for a 'full and fair'[1] balance sheet to be distributed at annual general meetings, and the concept of auditing was introduced.

---

1 The term 'full and fair' was first mentioned in relation to balance sheets and reporting in the Joint Stock Companies Act 1844, passed during the railway mania. The accounting debate around what precisely constitutes 'full and fair' (or, later, 'true and fair'), and how such a requirement might be enforced, has been ongoing ever since.

The crisis cycle

However the problem with simply telling companies to 'tell it like it is' was that business itself was advancing and complexifying at pace. This constantly created new openings as to how exactly companies could 'tell it', while accounting standards and reporting regulations were always running to catch up. Consequently, misleading information could still be fed to shareholders, thus setting the conditions for further shock collapses, regulatory backlashes, and thereby, a full crisis cycle (see figure 1).

Figure 1. The crisis cycle that fashioned the annual report

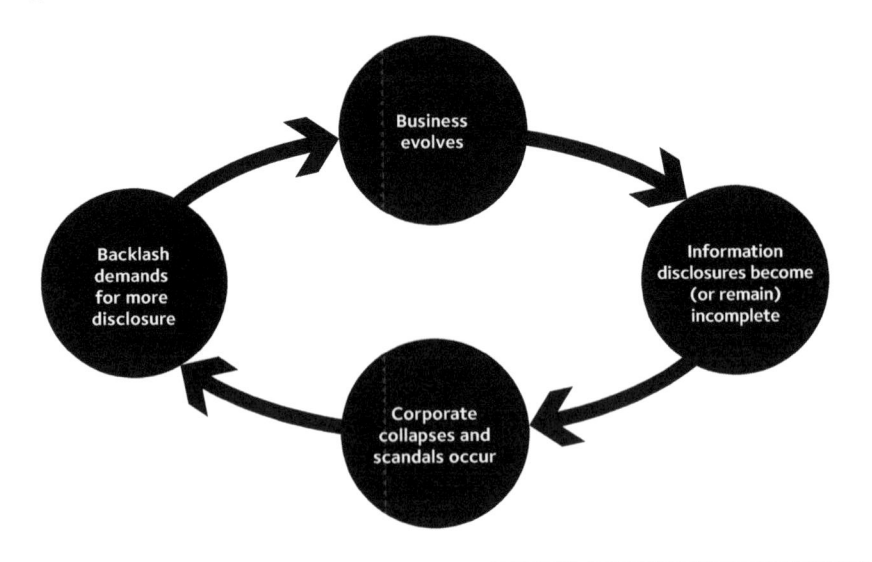

Business evolves → Information disclosures become (or remain) incomplete → Corporate collapses and scandals occur → Backlash demands for more disclosure → (Business evolves)

Within a few decades of the railway scandal, a full cycle had been completed. In 1868, the City of Glasgow Bank collapsed – scandalously – and a raft of new accounting specifications, industry standards, and enhanced tools for auditing, all followed.

Over the century-and-a-half since, companies, shareholders and governments have been going round and round, and it is through such rounds of the cycle that the annual report, and all the regulatory bodies and accounting standards that underpin it, have been fashioned into their current form, and continue to be fashioned.

1990s to today: recent rounds of the crisis cycle and how they define the current report

Here are the last few crisis cycle incidents that have given us the reporting structure we're now familiar with:

- In the early 1990s, a series of high-profile scandals, including the collapse of BCCI and Robert Maxwell's companies, led to a new set of governance recommendations. These were laid out in the Cadbury Report (1992) and formed the basis of what is now the governance section of the annual report.
- The global financial crisis of 2008-09 was followed first by the Walker Review (2009), which recommended a new set of banking regulations, and then by the Companies Act 2006 (Strategic Report and Directors' Report) Regulations 2013, which introduced the strategic report section of the annual report.
- The collapse of BHS in 2016 and then Carillion in 2018, among others, further fuelled the drive to produce renewed Guidance on the Strategic Report (2018), a new UK Corporate Governance Code (2018),[1] and, most significantly perhaps, the Kingman Review (2018). Under the Kingman Review's recommendations, the Financial Reporting Council (FRC) is to be replaced by a considerably more powerful Audit, Reporting and Governance Authority (ARGA). The stated aim of creating ARGA is to increase the accountability of companies for their reporting, and to improve the quality and independence of auditing. But, despite further high-profile collapses – Patisserie Valerie and Thomas Cook in 2019, for example, or Wirecard in 2020 – we are still, in late 2021, waiting for this to come about.

More regulations, more auditing... *plus ça change, plus c'est la même chose...*

---

1 The new code, in its introduction, is clear about how it became: 'as a result of financial crises and high-profile examples of inadequate governance and misconduct, which have led to poor outcomes for a wide range of stakeholders.' *The UK Corporate Governance Code* (2018), p.1.

What the history of reporting tells us
This has been a whistle-stop history of the annual report, but there are two important points to draw from it:

1. **More, more, more:** Though cyclical in motion, the higher-level direction of travel is one way: from less disclosure to more. The annual report has gone from the one-pager of the 1600s to the 200-odd pager of 2021, and though there have been flat periods along the way, there have been no significant dips. Reports don't get shorter, nor does the audit scope narrow.[1]

2. **The reluctant reporter:** Companies don't volunteer 'full and fair' reporting spontaneously or naturally. Rather, the progression towards the extensive disclosures that make up the annual reports of today has been driven primarily by external demands and statutes, themselves driven by market failures and public outcries. Companies for their part have moved to meet these demands with varying degrees of alacrity, but in so doing, have been primarily reactive. (This is notably different from, say, the history of product innovation, which has been driven much more by companies themselves.)[2]

Reporting's inherent conflict of interest
It is further worth noting that both of these points could probably have been predicted given the essential dynamics that produced reporting in the first place (see figure 2).

---

[1] With requirements to report against the Task Force on Climate-related Financial Disclosures coming into force for premium-listed companies in 2021-22, we can say with confidence that the growth of the annual report isn't done yet.

[2] Sustainability reporting, it could be argued, has to date been driven less by statutory regulation. However, true to the crisis cycle, it has been greatly driven by a series of social and environmental disasters, backlashes and sustained external pressure, with companies again playing a primarily reactive role (more on this below under 'The wider stakeholder'). More formal regulation of sustainability reporting is on the way, as discussed in Chapter 2.

Figure 2. The essential dynamics of reporting

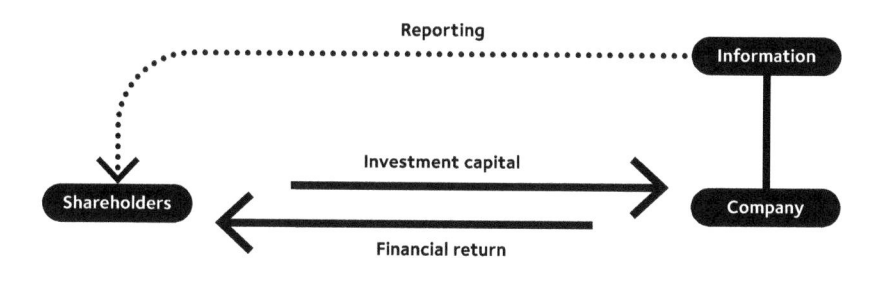

```
                        Reporting
      ·······································    Information
      :                                              |
      :                                              |
      ▼           Investment capital                 |
  ┌─────────┐    ──────────────────────▶      ┌──────────┐
  │Share-   │                                  │ Company  │
  │holders  │    ◀──────────────────────       │          │
  └─────────┘        Financial return          └──────────┘
```

According to this model, the company provides shareholders[1] with a financial return in exchange for use of their capital and, alongside it, the reporting that informs that capital. However, in this exchange, the information lies all on the side of the company. And as a result:

1. Shareholders have relatively limited means of knowing if the reports they are being given are accurate and complete – hence the continuous requests for more and more disclosure and auditing (see point 1 above).

2. Companies, on the other side, when preparing their reports, are faced with an obvious conflict of interest. If the information is all positive, then the conflict is low; but if things are a little less glowing, then a company's short-term interests at least, assuming it still wants the shareholders' capital, may well lie in it being less than wholly transparent. And, since all companies know that things are never always all glowing, they may be reluctant, even in good years, to disclose more than they have to as this only sets a precedent. Consequently, companies are naturally somewhat disclosure-shy – hence their more passive role in this

---

1 Shareholders are traditionally the direct recipients of the annual report, but at core, the concept is that the report informs the investment market at large, and guides its ability to value shares accurately (hence the practice of publishing the report, which has been a convention since the development of listing requirements and sophisticated reporting in the nineteenth century). I've continued to use the term 'shareholder' here and in the argument as it develops below, but the 'shareholder' can be taken to stand in for the investment community at large, including institutional and retail investors, funds, investment analysts, advisers, agents, etc.

history, and the perennial risk of reporting drifting away from reality, giving rise in turn to shock failures and outcries (see point 2 above).

In formal terms, this relationship between shareholders and companies is described as a 'lack of goal congruence'. Or to propose a less formal analogy, the company being asked to report on its own performance could be seen as the little girl being asked to mark her own homework. Add to this the fact that companies – quite legitimately – don't want to give anything away to their competitors, and it becomes the little girl being asked not only to mark her own homework, but also share it with the rest of the class.

In short, an inevitable tension exists between shareholders' desire for companies to tell them the whole truth, and companies' tendency to tell them a little bit less than that. The tension is structural, and the result for reporting is a spectrum that ranges from fair to fraudulent, and on which all annual reports sit (see figure 3).

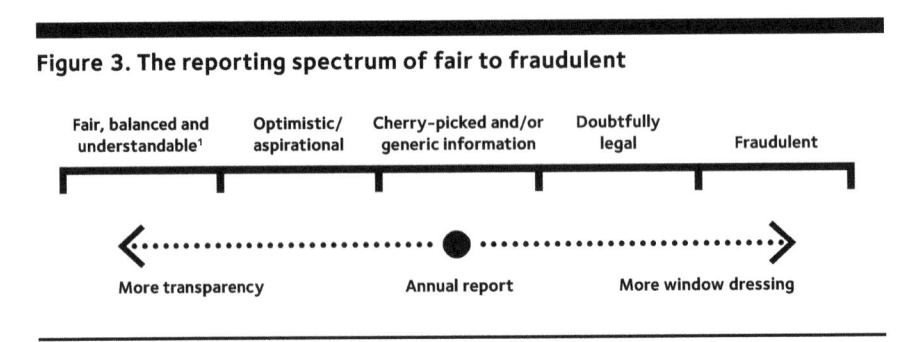

Figure 3. The reporting spectrum of fair to fraudulent

| Fair, balanced and understandable[1] | Optimistic/ aspirational | Cherry-picked and/or generic information | Doubtfully legal | Fraudulent |

← More transparency ··· Annual report ··· More window dressing →

An uncomfortable conversation – but one worth having

For companies preparing their annual reports, the question of where on this spectrum they want to sit is an important one – both for reporting strategy and for basic self-understanding. It is one, however, that in practice doesn't get a lot of airtime. Why?

---

1 This is the FRC's current wording for asking companies, in their reporting, essentially to 'tell it like it is'. Over the years, companies have had much the same request put to them in numerous different forms (having been told, variously, to be 'full and fair', 'true and correct', 'fair and balanced', 'true and fair', 'fair, balanced and understandable', etc.) by numerous different regulatory and accounting bodies as they all, following each round of the crisis cycle, nervously reshuffle their adjectives.

The simple answer is that it's uncomfortable. People don't like to be suspected of dishonesty, much less, to have to question their own honesty, and for companies working on their annual reports, it is far preferable to operate under the premise that they are only ever trying to do the right thing in a complex and competitive world. Communications or reporting teams may struggle to be as fully 'fair, balanced and understandable' as they'd like and, lacking the leverage to change everything in their companies, find themselves window dressing a little more than ideal – even if it's 'just for now' or 'just on these one or two things'. They may even window dress their own window dressing to themselves because, after all, we're all human, and naturally prefer to make ourselves look nice. Meanwhile external parties, such as auditors and reporting agencies, may (unsurprisingly) be reluctant to upset their clients. They probably don't challenge them as much as they should (see the box 'Is audit broken' below, and Chapter 5 for more on agencies), and indeed, just throwing around a term like 'window dressing' in a book like this may not be all that welcome.

However the reason I am doing so is because not to would be to ignore the elephant in the reporting team meeting room. It would require a denial of both the history of reporting and the contemporary reality that a lot of it continues to be characterised by spin, boilerplate, clutter, whitewash, greenwash, obfuscation and so on. All are prominent features of today's reporting landscape, and everybody knows it – you need only look at what they're saying (see figure 4).

Figure 4. Corporate reporting under suspicion

38% of investors trust the information companies report enough to make decisions

50% of people in the UK trust business 'to do what's right'

"In fact almost nothing is being done apart from **clever accounting** and **creative PR**"
– Greta Thunberg, *Time* Person of the Year 2019

And then compare it with what directors and auditors are saying (see figure 5).

Figure 5. Corporate reporting held in high confidence; compare with figure 4 for the perception gap between company directors and auditors and the readers of their reports

91% of company directors have high levels of confidence in the quality of corporate reporting

95% of auditors have the same confidence

IS AUDIT BROKEN?

The question of whether auditors are too much in the pocket of company directors has been present ever since the concept of auditing came about in the 1840s. A major recommendation of the recent Kingman Review (2018) is to increase regulation of audit firms, and to address the issue of concentration in the industry. The 'Big 4' firms – Deloitte, EY, KPMG and PwC – all date back to the 1840s to 1870s period when auditing was born. By 2018, they accounted for 100% of FTSE 100 audits and 98% of FTSE 350 audits. It is probably safe to say they have not achieved such levels of longevity and ultimate dominance by going out of their way to alienate the firms they work for (though they have, over that time, repeatedly signed off on the reports of companies that, less than 12 months later, 'scandalously' collapsed). The 2019 report of the Competition and Markets Authority recommended the separation of audit from consulting services, and the introduction of statutory regulatory powers to increase the accountability of companies' audit committees. The Brydon Review (also 2019) took the position that, 'Audit is not broken but it has lost its way...'

The tensions that pull reports both left and right on the spectrum, towards either more transparency or more window dressing, are fundamental and perennial. The argument can always be made that, from the perspective of the market, transparency is better, and companies as a whole will reap their rewards in the form of improved access to capital at lower cost. This may not, however, be enough to convince an individual company that's having a tough year not to lean right on the spectrum, nor inspire one having an average year to break left, especially when all its peers are in a huddle in the middle.

What may also be happening here is that individual companies that are dealing with the inescapably difficult task of reporting (and doing so in the context of inherent conflicts of interest, shifting regulations, and the simple pressure of getting on with business at the same time), award themselves the benefit of the doubt when looking upon gaps here and there in their reports. They are of course conscious of all the good work that has gone in, and all the good things that, in the end, were left out. Investors however, when coming to the report from outside, will see none of this. Instead they will be highly conscious of the disastrous possibility that they are being misled, and will read therefore not with the benefit of the doubt, but with a suspicious eye. This is an extension of the information asymmetry noted above (figure 2), and one that may well be contributing to the perception gap (figures 4 and 5).

All this makes for dour reading perhaps, but there are useful takeaways. First, for companies, is the deep-level realisation that they are under suspicion. Moreover, if they can find the courage to suspect themselves, and have the uncomfortable conversation, they will get much closer to the perspective of their readers. This can yield useful insights. For example, if company directors and secretaries start to read their own reports with a suspicious eye, it becomes immediately obvious that a lack of information can look like evasion. Elsewhere: formulaic or generic content looks like cover up; using different figures and examples every year looks like cherry-picking; and bland positives followed only by vagueness and murk look all too much like the infamous bubble company that was *'carrying on an undertaking of great advantage, but nobody to know what it is'*.

EXERCISE

Reading with a suspicious eye

As a company, ask yourself: how believed are you? Don't just give yourself a pass – try to think critically, and read with a suspicious eye. How believed were you last year? What responses did you get to last year's report, and where on the spectrum would you place it?

It's difficult to be objective when you are close to the material, so start with a competitor:

- try reading a competitor's report with a suspicious eye
- find the sections that look unconvincing to you
- return to your own report and compare; are there weaknesses?

Invite suspicion as a means to test how robust your reporting is. Have the courage to have the uncomfortable conversation – both internally and with your agency, if you use one. Remember that your readers are there to scrutinise your reporting, not to swallow it, and that if you want to speak to them, you'll have to start to think like them.

> **THE RISK OF SILENCE: AN EXAMPLE**
> Between 2017 and 2019, 65% of FTSE 350 companies changed one or more of their key performance indicators (KPIs). However in most cases it is unclear why, because they are silent on this subject (that there has been a change can only be divined by comparing two years' worth of reports). What could be the reason? Has the company strategy changed, requiring new measures and therefore KPIs? Or have better measures been found for tracking progress towards the same objectives? Or are these companies simply picking, from one year to the next, whichever numbers look better? Reading with a suspicious eye, and in the absence of any other explanation, it looks like the last.

A second (but in fact primary) reader of your report: you

Reports are primarily thought of as being for shareholders, and indeed it was the emergence of shareholders as readers that provided the impetus for companies to start writing reports. However for thousands of years before that, businesses had been collecting and organising financial information so they could read it themselves. Indeed those that did this effectively were the ones that were able to reality-check their strategies, and thereby make better decisions and outcompete the rest – which is how technologies like writing and accounting caught on in the first place. Properly speaking, therefore, a report's primary readers should be its writers.

It follows that for companies, a perhaps counterintuitive advantage of having shareholders – and with them, demands for extensive, detailed, high-quality reporting – is that it forces those companies to report extensively, in detail, with quality, etc. *to themselves*. This self-reporting is in fact something that as people we are notoriously bad at. We are all riddled with bias, and have a tendency to focus more on the things we want to, while pushing to one side this or that ominous piece of paper or unappetising possibility, and leaving booking that dentist appointment for later... For these reasons, accountability is generally a good in and of itself, even on the individual level. We are all better managers of ourselves when there's someone else watching over us.

Companies are no different, and as they and their groups become ever larger and more complex, the benefit of having an annual process that gathers together all current, material information – welcome and unwelcome – in a single document of record, becomes greater and greater. Annual reports enable segmented departments to share information and improve their basic awareness of each other, and give department leaders an opportunity to provide crucial feedback. And while companies do of course have internal reporting mechanisms for precisely these purposes, the fact that the annual report is published gives it extra potency through that special, someone-watching-over-me effect. This can be particularly beneficial for directors, who may rarely write their own reports, but do, we hope, read them. After all, they have to sign them off.

The directors as readers — and responders

Thinking of the directors as readers presents an intriguing danger for companies that drift right on the 'fair to fraudulent' spectrum. Internal pressure on reports to be overly positive can lead to results that fail to convince the suspicious eyes of shareholders; however directors may be less quick to challenge – and more liable to be persuaded by – their own aspirational rhetoric and cherry-picked examples. This can lead to directors forming unrealistic views both of their own companies and of how they are being perceived. The situation is a little like a man who commissions a flattering portrait of himself, and then, hanging the result in his dining room, comes to believe too much in the likeness (see the perception gap of figures 4 and 5 above).

Conversely, for those companies that bravely steer left on the spectrum, and include challenging information in their reports, there is the added bonus that this will grab the attention of directors, and empower them to respond. This is of course the essence of knowledge management, and is precisely why shareholders say they find companies who report challenges, and how they are dealing with them, far more convincing than those who discuss only successes. For the canny investor, a good report – meaning a transparent, warts-and-all one – is a proxy for good management (i.e. well-informed, intelligent, responsive).

The report tail wagging the company dog

That reporting can actually encourage better management and corporate governance has not been lost on regulators – ironically perhaps given that many companies remain unconvinced. Nevertheless, it is for this reason that, as regulatory requirements have advanced over the years, they have expanded massively in their remit. From the report's initial focus only on balance sheets and past financial performance, requirements now encompass a wide-ranging overview of policies, processes and future company strategy. The core theory at work is that if companies have to report on all these things to others, then they have in some way to address them for themselves.

Companies now, for example, have to report on trends and risks, which means they have to come up with some, and plan for them. Likewise, companies have to report on KPIs, meaning they have to set and track some; and on governance measures, meaning they have to devise and implement some; and so on. According to this, regulators can effectively define whatever they think companies should do, and then simply by obliging them to write about it, they can drive its adoption. By a curious twist, the communication leads the action, or, the tail wags the dog.

In reality, multinational corporations are big dogs, and annual reports small tails.[1] The mutt won't wag so easily, and as soon as something like company strategy or risk planning becomes nothing but a reporting team discussion, we're clearly veering right on the fair to fraudulent spectrum. Even so, the tail may be able to send a signal to the dog. What has been window dressed for the report this year, but flagged, may get more attention from directors next year. It's a gradual process.

---

[1] The FRC is being replaced as a regulator of auditors, accountants and actuaries, and overseer of corporate reporting, largely because it failed to wag corporate behaviour sufficiently vigorously to prevent another round of the crisis cycle – i.e. the collapse of Carillion in 2018 and others (see above). In the subsequent fall out, a report from Parliament's Business Select Committee described the FRC as 'chronically passive' and 'too timid' (www.theguardian.com/business/2019/mar/11/audit-watchdogs-leaders-quit-in-overhaul-after-scandals). Whether or not the souped-up replacement regulator, ARGA, will do any better is, at the time of writing, to be seen. It is hard however to imagine ARGA becoming the dog, and Royal Dutch Shell or HSBC, for example, the tail.

Write the report you need to read
But regulatory pointers as to all the things a company should be thinking about (which fill up reporting checklists) should really be something of an aside. The core benefit of a company conceiving of itself as the reader of its own report is that it can learn those things about its own operations that it most needs to know. Reporting should in essence be a 'know thyself' – or *nosce te ipsum* – process. By this, the company leverages the need to write for others as a means to write to itself, and thereby genuinely articulate: what is and isn't working; how capital is being used; what the outcomes are, and how these compare with the strategy; where there are knowledge gaps; and so on. When gathering information for a report, always ask yourself: what do we need to know as a business, and, how can we make our own decisions better informed? Then use the report as a tool to get those answers. Companies that write the reports they need to read are winning a valuable trick here (to gauge how well you're doing, see the exercise on the next page).

A third reader of your report: the wider stakeholder
Companies and shareholders have long been the dominant parties when it comes to reporting, but a third has surfaced more recently as having an interest: the 'wider stakeholders'. This is a group that roughly comprises current and potential employees, customers, suppliers, affected communities and, to some extent, society at large.

That companies affect other people has always been apparent, and indeed was a key driver of governmental involvement in reporting in the first place. As over the years companies have got bigger, the number of people affected has grown, to the extent that with the large multinationals of today, these wider stakeholder groups now run well into the millions and reach all around the world. At such scale, they have come to exert a distinct political force of their own. What's more, because this is the information age, wider stakeholders are considerably better informed than ever before; they're also louder, because they have social media; and they're more demanding, because that's what happens when people both know more and have a voice to talk about it. The era when companies could just go about their business and expect stakeholders to fall in line is over.

EXERCISE

Are you writing the report you need to read?

YES	NO
senior leadership is meaningfully involved in preparing the report	report is predominantly a reporting team project with sign-off from senior leadership
report regarded as a valuable internal process	report regarded as either a PR document or a regulatory tick-box exercise
discussion and key figures in the report match those used in Board meetings	discussion and key figures in the report are only ever seen in the annual report
there is meaningful feedback on the report from leadership and the company as a whole	reporting team receive little or no substantive feedback
learning drives new decisions	nothing to learn here

None of this is altogether new. Wider stakeholders first started swimming up into company consciousness in response to the changing political climate of the 1960s, when activism and mass protest movements started to capture the public mood. Notably, the association of Dow Chemicals with napalm and the Vietnam War, and the strongly negative public response, provided an early example of how the crowd could turn against a company, and wreak reputational damage. Spurred into action, companies started publishing social responsibility disclosures, and these have since evolved into the sustainability, or environmental, social and governance (ESG), reporting of today.

This evolutionary process has been significantly driven by a kind of sustainability crisis cycle (operating in parallel to the crisis cycle discussed above), with a loop again featuring corporate disasters, public outrage and backlash, and a response of more and more reporting. Notable crises include the Bhopal toxic gas leak of 1984 and the Exxon Valdez oil spill of 1989, both of which triggered significant stakeholder outcries, and then reporting responses, and contributed to the gradual establishment of external standard-setting bodies, such as the Global Reporting Initiative (GRI). Or on another front, the slow realisation of a climate crisis, and again, growing stakeholder demand, led to the establishment, among others, of the Climate Standards Disclosure Board (CSDB) and its recent Task Force on Climate-related Financial Disclosures (TCFD). These bodies develop standards for more sustainability disclosure, which cycle round into pressure on companies to meet these standards (reporting against TCFD is now a requirement for UK premium-listed companies) – much like how financial accounting standards were developed a century-and-a-half (and more) earlier.

However, while wider stakeholder awareness has been in motion since the 1960s, things have recently become a lot more intense. The number of companies directly addressing stakeholder engagement in their annual reports skyrocketed almost overnight, in reporting terms, from 26% in 2017-18 to 82% in 2018-19 (no doubt prompted by the fact that regulation was about to come in to tell them to do just that). Companies are now suddenly scrambling to appear more 'stakeholder-woke', and are talking about their 'social licence to operate' with a genuine fear that they might lose it.

Governments are equally keen to appear 'woke', and for their part have been active in the way they know best: through more regulation. Again, as with financial reporting, the statutory side follows a little after, but that it is arriving on the stakeholder and sustainability front is beyond question. In the UK, a recent set of changes to reporting around section 172 of the Companies Act 2006 now obliges company directors to make a specific statement about how, when carrying out their duties, they 'have regard' for wider stakeholders – listed as employees, customers, suppliers, communities and the environment. And moreover, directors of large companies must further report annually on the effect of that regard on 'the principal decisions taken by the company.'

From shareholder to stakeholder...
This is particularly significant because it shifts the very concept of what a company is and does. Having once been an entity that was essentially expected to make money for shareholders, while letting everything else take care of itself, companies are now being told they have to create 'enlightened shareholder value' – meaning that they should make money for shareholders as well as good stuff for everyone else, and without wrecking the planet too, please. Roll over Milton Friedman.

The effect of all this on reporting is sure to be further travel in the inexorable direction of more and more disclosure. In the near-to-medium future, it is likely that statutory requirements around wider stakeholder and sustainability matters will become more focused, more granular, and include increasing levels of auditing. Indeed the current mandatory statements[1] look like being early markers on a journey towards a fully standardised system of social and environmental accounting (more on this in Chapter 2).

However, what all this regard for, and disclosure about, wider stakeholders doesn't address is the matter of actually reporting *to* them. Yet not to think about this would be a significant miss – not least because they probably, if somewhat surprisingly, make up the majority of readers of the reports of large companies. If you think about it, wider stakeholders clearly should make up the majority, given the sheer number there are out there, but because of the framework we are all so familiar with

---

1 For example around modern slavery, gender pay gap, employee pay ratios, energy use and CO_2 emissions.

(i.e. the shareholder-company relationship shown in figure 2 above), it's something many companies are still struggling to take on board. Nevertheless, the numbers are overwhelming (see figure 6).

Figure 6. Readers of the annual report[1]

48% of report readers identify as current, potential or past employees

27% identify as customers

6% identify as institutional investors

...and what that means for the annual report

What do these percentages tell us? For one, certainly, that a narrow focus on share price, dividends and financials – even imagining that's all shareholders care about which, given the clamour for ESG information is clearly an outdated assumption – is going to satisfy only a minority of readers (even if a very important minority, and one that uses the annual report as a document of record). But this only plucks on the next question, which is: What are all these other people, if they don't own shares, picking up the report for? There is no single answer (wider stakeholders are a diverse lot), but the common thread running through all their interests will be a desire to read the company's story. This means things like: What does the company as a whole actually do? How does it operate? What are its values and purpose? How does it treat people? How is or isn't it contributing to solving the climate crisis? What is it planning on doing next? And what does all this mean for me, the stakeholder? What role in this story do I – or might I – play? People who work for a company (or are thinking about it), buy from that company (or are thinking about it), or are being affected by that company in some way,

---

[1] These figures are from Radley Yeldar, *The Battle For Annual Reporting* (2019), p.8. Conclusive data about annual report readership is notoriously difficult to come by as reports are mostly downloaded as PDFs, with many companies recording little more than download numbers. Radley Yeldar's results come from a study of over 1,000 informed citizens, business leaders, analysts and investors.

genuinely want to know. And the fact that they are now coming to the annual report to find out presents the company with a golden opportunity – both to provide answers, and control the narrative.

In an increasingly stakeholder-conscious world, a company's ability to communicate successfully about these issues in their annual report and elsewhere will become ever more critical (for more on reporting outside the annual report see Chapter 2). It will indubitably influence the company's ability to attract and retain talent (the 48% above), as well as customers (the 27%), with both factors clearly playing into future share price. This even suggests a role for reporting in the battleground of competitive advantage, with companies vying to out-report each other not only on financial numbers but also on narrative excellence.

The clear danger here is that reporting becomes an all-out PR effort, and again veers right on the fair-to-fraudulent spectrum. However companies would do well to remember that most stakeholders are every bit as mistrustful as shareholders, and will read reports with the same suspicious eye. Companies that try for save-the-world stories, but end up with content that is vague, incoherent or implausible, reap more reputational harm than good. All the more reason then to get the story straight. ■

PART II

Getting your story straight

AN ANNUAL REPORT, first and foremost, should be useful to its readers. It should inform:

- **shareholders** about how their capital is being used, the value that is being created, and the value (therefore) of the investment itself
- **companies** about those things they most need to know about themselves, and their operations and strategy, thus acting as a tool for knowledge management
- **wider stakeholders** about the nature and character of the business.

To serve any of these readers well, the report needs to be true and meaningful. Much of the above has been about telling the truth, but a checklist of true information isn't of itself meaningful. To speak to us, it needs to be woven into a story, which requires technique. So now for the technique.

Telling a story
The word 'story' gets bandied around a lot when people are working on annual reports, but without much clarity about what it's being used to mean. Here's a fairly typical conversation a reporting agency copywriter might have with a corporate client.
COMPANY X: We need the text to tell our story.
WRITER: OK, great. What's your story?
COMPANY X: [*Blank faces all round.*] You're the writer. Isn't that your job?

The short answer is, 'No,' although the longer answer, which the writer is more likely to offer, will probably be closer to, 'I can ask you the right questions, and help you find the right words, but it still needs to be your story.'

However they get on, what is certain is that if it's an agency hired gun that is actually thinking up the story in its entirety, as opposed to helping the company write it in a way that their audiences will understand, it's going to be window dressing (just as much as if the writer is thinking up the strategy, the business model, or anything else significant in the report). Agencies are there to express things well, and keep the report on message, not create the message (more on working with agencies in Chapter 5).

But this still leaves the existential question of what the message is. Companies can go into deep soul-searching here, with or without consultants to hold their hands, but much of what we see tends to be insipid. I've come across, as acting proxies for a company story: 'We focus on creating value for stakeholders,' 'We unlock future potential,' 'We find better solutions,' and even, 'We care.' Can you guess what any of these companies even do? Obviously not.

What actually is a story?
The reason why such efforts fail is because of a fundamental misunderstanding of what a story really is. We all learn about stories early in life, and so it's easy to assume we know what they are, but, because for the most part we don't decompose them into parts, we're often left blank when suddenly we have to build one ourselves. It's not so obvious, we discover, and therefore worth spending a little time on here.

The essential mechanics of a story are: action set in context (see figure 7).

Figure 7. The essential mechanics of a story

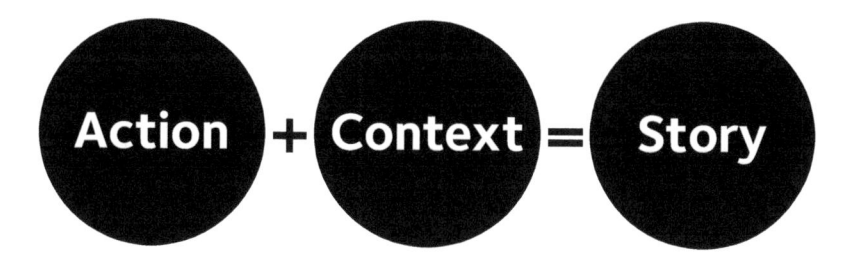

Action + Context = Story

That's a little abstract though, so here's an example.
- **Action:** A man spends ten years at sea
- **Context:** The Trojan War comes to an end and the Greeks head back
- **Story:** At the end of the Trojan war, Odysseus sets sail for home. However his ship is blown off course, and he spends the next ten years at sea, encountering many dangers and obstacles before finally reaching Ithaca, where he is reunited with his beloved wife and son.

There are a number of interesting things to be said about each of these elements and how they combine. It's actually easiest to deal with the context first, so let's do it in that order (and then look at how it all relates to a company doing business).

Context
The context provides the *why* of the story. It makes sense of it. Why was Odysseus at sea? Because he'd been at the Trojan War. Where was he trying to go? Home to see his wife and son. The context allows us to put ourselves in Odysseus' position, and convince ourselves of the logic of his action. We can say, *'Ah yes, if I were there, that's what I'd do'* – but we can only imagine being there if we know enough about the context.

Key here is that the contextual information supplied is relevant to the action being described. In the ultra-short version of *The Odyssey* given above, we only need enough context to provide purpose to the ten years at sea. What we do not need are high-level generic statements about the context, such as: 'The ancient world provided an attractive market for heroism.' Nor do we need spurious detail, such as a

360-degree appraisal of the risks of wearing a tunic at sea. Indeed Homer's supreme skill in writing the epic version of *The Odyssey* is that he gives us precisely the information we need (and not more) at each stage to be Odysseus in our own minds.

Action
The action is what Odysseus is doing, plain and simple. In both the ultra-short version and the full epic poem, the focus is on what's happening. Again, it is not absurdly abstracted – for example, we're not told, 'Odysseus is committed to creating well-being value for his family'. Nor is it a dreary recitation of policy mechanics, such as, 'Odysseus set in place quality reviewing systems to ensure best practice navigational standards were rigorously maintained at all times'. Instead we're told about the decisions Odysseus makes, the actions he takes, and how these work out.

Story
The magical addition of 'action plus context' relies on the two relating to each other in a clear and tangible fashion. Just as you can't add apples and bananas, you can't add an ancient Greek at sea with, say, the topography of Uzbekistan. The two have to lock together. A further important point to note is that when they do add nicely, the story that results has a natural beginning, middle and end. Odysseus starts by leaving Troy behind, then does a bunch of stuff at sea, and finally arrives at home. This structure ensures that all the well-known episodes within the story – the Cyclops, the sirens, Scylla and Charybdis, and so on – all take place within a clear master narrative.[1]

How to relate all this to an annual report

All very helpful if you're an epic poet, you may say, but what if you're a company secretary wrestling with an annual report? Well the analogy should, I hope, be relatively clear. Odysseus is the company, the action is what the company is doing, and the context is the company's business environment.

---

1 In *The Odyssey*, Homer actually plays around with the timeline a fair bit. He makes extensive use of recounted episodes, and the narrative shifts several times back and forth to Ithaca, where Penelope and Telemachus are dealing with the suitors. However this free movement within the story is only possible because the master narrative, with its beginning, middle and end, is so clear.

By this, the context includes things like market trends and factors, risks and uncertainties, and social and environmental matters. The key feature of these, as pointed out above, is that they are all relevant to the action. Relevance in corporate reporting speak is *materiality*, and the true test of the materiality of a piece of information is that it informs the decisions the company is making, and the actions it is therefore pursuing. I.e. it makes the actions make sense – or, from the reader's point of view – it enables the reader to put him or herself in the company's position, see the logic, and think, *'Ah yes, if I were there, that's what I'd do'*.

From this, rather neatly, the strategy emerges, since the strategy is simply the logic of what the company is doing, and how it's going about doing it, in relation to the context. Given a particular business context, the company pursues a set of actions, and these are strategic by virtue of having a clear and tangible relationship with that context. This sets the framework for the company's strategic management, and as it further follows that these actions will lead to something, following them logically should take you to the objectives, and ultimately, the high-level vision or purpose — i.e. the final *why* of the story.

Finding your beginning, middle and end
Notably, all of this falls out just from the combination of the company's actions and its context. The final part of the magical addition that makes the story is then establishing the beginning, middle and end. Here things are marginally trickier than in *The Odyssey*, where Homer had the advantage of writing after Odysseus had made it home, and the journey was complete. For a company coming up to its year end, the story isn't quite finished – or at least we hope not – and the report itself, instead of being like *The Odyssey* in its entirety, is perhaps more like a single episode within, let's say, *Odyssey: The Netflix Series*. It is the latest instalment within the bigger story of the company's ongoing existence.

However, for a Netflix series to be successful, every individual episode must equally have a beginning, middle and end. There is the master narrative that provides the frame (in the case of *The Odyssey*, this is the journey back to Ithaca), and then the episodes focus on the details of one or another particular encounter along the way, and how they were navigated (e.g. the Cyclops, the Sirens, etc.).

For a company report, the 'episode' is the financial year. What the company has been doing over the course of that year – the challenges it has faced, and how it has managed them – provides the action, and this should again relate to the context, and speak to the strategy. A further important point is the use of KPIs, which track the progress being made through that action (the equivalent, let's say, of nautical miles sailed along the planned route back to Ithaca). And then to ensure these KPIs are not just measures in the air, we need some targets (let's say, 100 miles sailed by the year end).

Helpfully all this produces a beginning, middle and end by itself, as the beginning is simply the position of the company at the start of the year; the middle, performance over the course of the year, as demonstrated by results against the KPIs; and the end, the analysis of those results in relation to the targets, plus any consequent adjustments to the strategy that need to be made when looking at next year and beyond. If the strategy is much the same, the KPIs can be expected to stay, and only the targets get updated; if the strategy changes, this most likely requires new KPIs and targets. And reciprocally, if the KPIs change, this necessarily implies that there has been a change in strategy (in which case, this needs to be explained), or that a new, better tracker of progress has been found (in which case, this also needs to be explained).[1] Then the final proof of it all is that delivery on the KPIs and targets (or lack of it) is appropriately reflected in executive pay, as set out in the remuneration section (more on this below in 'On the governance and remuneration sections').

Flow

The most important point here, and for the telling of an effective story, is the extent to which all of this flows together. There is a continuous movement throughout the company's actions, strategy and context, which follows through into the KPIs, targets and performance, and on into remuneration and the consequent strategy – or plan of action – for next year. Everything is connected.

---

[1] See p.29 'The risk of silence: an example.' According to the logic of storytelling, that most companies between 2017 and 2019 year both changed their KPIs, and didn't say why, is a major fail.

A secondary point, for the writing of an annual report, is the extent to which all of this maps across to the statutory requirements for the strategic report, which is the main home of the company story. To some extent this is unsurprising as the development of the strategic report itself, as a reporting requirement, was very much driven by the concept of narrative reporting, and in its guidance on how to write one, the FRC repeatedly exhorts companies to 'tell their story'. Happy the result then that the main 'contents elements' diagram from the FRC Guidance matches the elements of good storytelling just as I've laid them out (see figure 8)!

Figure 8. Telling a story with the FRC contents list[1]

STRATEGIC MANAGEMENT How the entity generates and preserves value	**BUSINESS ENVIRONMENT** The internal and external environment in which the entity operates	**BUSINESS PERFORMANCE AND POSITION** How the entity has developed and performed and its position at the year end
• Strategy • Business model	• Trends and factors • Principal risks and uncertainties • Environmental, employee, social, community and human rights matters	• Analysis of performance and position • Key performance indicators (KPIs) • Employee gender diversity (required disclosure)
This must talk about what the company is actually doing, and how its actions relate to the context. The strategy is the embedded logic of this relationship, and following the strategy to its logical conclusions defines the objectives and high-level purpose. The business model then sets the 'master narrative' for the company's ongoing operations.	This provides the contextual information for readers to be able to put themselves in the company's position, and think, *'Ah yes, if I were there, that's what I'd do.'* It makes sense of the action. Key is that the information – on trends, factors, risks, uncertainties and social and environmental matters – is all relevant, or *material*, meaning that it relates in a clear and tangible fashion to the actions and strategy of the company. Especially relevant is how the context is evolving, and the strategy responding.	This provides information on performance this year – i.e. if the plan of action, or strategy, was to achieve *x*, how much progress has been made? KPIs measure this progress, with targets to define good and bad performance. Analysis reflects on results in relation to the strategy, thus producing the strategy for next year, with appropriate KPIs and targets to measure progress on that.

---

1 The upper section of the diagram shows the contents elements of the strategic report, as displayed in the FRC *Guidance on the Strategic Report* (2018), p.25. The bottom row of boxes is my addition.

I started this chapter with the promise that I wasn't going to put a contents list before you, and I've partially violated that now. However my aim has been to demonstrate that if you begin by thinking about how to tell a story with your report, then the items on the contents checklist will take care of themselves. This is because the story naturally covers them. But the reverse is absolutely not true – i.e. if you set about ticking off the items on the contents checklist, then the story will not take care of itself. This is because what makes the story is the flow of sense from one item to the next, which a checklist approach, by its nature, will fail to achieve.

So tell your story already...
The problem annual reports have today is not one of compliance. Overwhelmingly companies comb through their checklists very effectively, and the number getting summoned by regulators is vanishingly small. However what companies are not doing well is telling stories that readers can read and believe.

Try telling the story of your own company report. Try doing it without referring to it, or any powerpoints or paragraphs of prepared text. Try talking through the story off the top of your head, and see if you can do it in two to three minutes without losing sense of what you're saying. A defining feature of a good story is that people can remember how it goes. This is because the flow of sense is natural and compelling.

Can you set out, as though to a friend, how the company strategy responds to the context and risks, and how that explains why the company has done what it's done this year? Can you point to the KPIs that evidence the results of those actions, and the targets that show the progress you're making? And can you further say how these results, and any other new developments this year, feed into what you're planning on doing next?

The two-minute story: yes you can

This may seem naive as an exercise, and companies can easily reply, 'We're extremely complex, and you're asking us to tell the story of our 182-page report in two to three minutes. It's impossible.' There are two responses to this. The first is that any story that is coherent can be reduced down to its essence, and told in ultra-short form. Companies that think they're too complex to explain themselves are in reality too muddled. The second is that two to three minutes of focused talk-time is roughly equivalent to ten minutes of reader-browsing time, which may well be about all you've got.

How long readers actually spend reading the annual report PDFs they've downloaded is anybody's guess.[1] What is certain though is that a small minority – perhaps 12% – read the report in full. The rest skip around, look for the bits they're interested in, and try to glean the main story. Most will probably be aiming to spend less than an hour on it, and for many, it will be a single-digit number of minutes. And it is probably safe to say that if even the writers of the report can't tell the story in minutes, its readers, given a similar timeframe, won't somehow be able to pull it out of the hat and tell it to themselves.

This is not to say the story should be reduced to a slogan and blazoned on every page. Slogans aren't stories, and as discussed above, usually tell readers nothing. Rather, the inner flow and logic of the report must be very clear to the people who are preparing it as they approach each individual section. If they know what the story is, then readers will be able to pick it up by skimming. If they don't, readers will be equally lost, and left wondering – as they so often are when faced by paragraph after paragraph of polished corporate text – *'Yes ok, but where are you going?'*

---

[1] See also Chapter 6 for how people use websites, and how much (or little) time they spend on web pages.

EXERCISE

A one-minute story, and three exercises

One time I was working on a large-scale writing project with someone who, late in the process, was gripped by a sudden fear that we'd left out an important piece of information. Was it there or not? He did a Ctrl+F search in the working document and, to his great delight, found it! It was buried in a paragraph on p.167 (who would have guessed?). He was greatly reassured to know that, from his perspective, it was in the document; however for a good 90% of readers, it might as well not have been. The problem was that it wasn't connected to anything, either in our minds or the work itself.

If we'd had our story straight, we wouldn't have had to use an electronic search; we'd simply have known that this piece of information, if present, would necessarily be connected to *that*, and would therefore sit *there*, in *that* particular section. In fact, what the exercise of thinking about it revealed was that we didn't sufficiently understand the core structure and inner logic of what we were working on.

Annual reports are long and complicated, and when knee-deep in preparing one or another section, such connection exercises, though simple, can be remarkably useful. They help you know if the thinking is truly joined-up at the high level, and if not, they point to what you need to do to fix it. And the great benefit then is that if you do fix it, the work you have to do at the knee-deep level becomes much clearer and faster.

Here are three such exercises for stress-testing the connectedness and logical flow of an annual report (to work alongside the two-minute story challenge on [page 47]).

CONNECTING THE FLOW: STRATEGY AND ACTION

- Take a piece of paper and write down in one column the five most significant things your company has done this year or that have affected it. These should reflect where the company's key resources (e.g. capital, employees, and the time, focus and energy of the Board) are being directed.
- Then in a second column, write down the strategy.

Do the two columns speak to each other? Is the relationship clear and tangible? If you covered one column with your hand, would you be able to guess what's in the other? If not, then the strategy is window dressing.

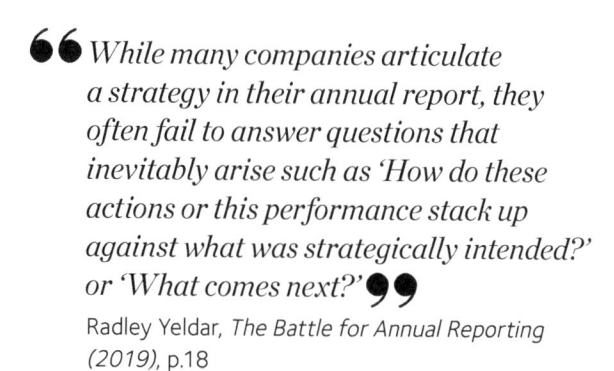

> *While many companies articulate a strategy in their annual report, they often fail to answer questions that inevitably arise such as 'How do these actions or this performance stack up against what was strategically intended?' or 'What comes next?'*
>
> Radley Yeldar, The Battle for Annual Reporting (2019), p.18

CONNECTING THE FLOW: CONTEXT AND MATERIALITY

- Take a piece of paper and write down in one column the risks and opportunities that you have defined as material to your business.
- Then in a second column, but as a separate process, write down the most significant things your company is doing or has done this year (like the first point of the exercise above, though go over five if need be).
- Try to match them up.

The relationships should again be clear and tangible. If the company is doing something that isn't responding to some material aspect of the context, then either you are not explaining something to your readers, or the action is senseless. If conversely there is a material risk or opportunity that isn't producing an action, then either there is a hole in the company strategy, or you are making a song and dance about something that you don't really care about.

> *If you look at their reporting, they've got a whole materiality process, and it's all very proper on paper. But then I went to a Board meeting, and I'd never seen a company so confused as to what it was about. The stuff in the report was a lot of smoke and mirrors. Materiality should be about knowing your own business.*
>
> Reflections of a senior manager and Board member

CONNECTING THE FLOW: KPIS AND PERFORMANCE

- Take a piece of paper and write down in one column the key points of your strategy.
- Then in a second column, but again as a separate process, write down your KPIs.
- Try to match them up.

Each point of the strategy should clearly relate to one or more KPIs, and those KPIs should be the things that tell you *better than anything else* about whether or not that point of the strategy is being delivered. As a thought experiment, imagine the results for each KPI going significantly up and down. Would that tangibly demonstrate that the strategy was succeeding brilliantly/failing horribly? (N.B. For this to work, the points of the strategy have to be specific; pale truisms like 'creating value for shareholders' are inadequate.)

If your strategy and KPIs are matched and working well together, then you can progress to part two of the exercise:

- Write down in a third column performance data on the KPIs (including this year, and the last 3-5 years where available).
- Write down in a fourth column last year's targets (i.e. the ones that were for this year).
- Write down in a fifth column the targets for next year.
- What story do the numbers tell you? Is what the performance data says about the delivery of the strategy faithfully reflected in the narrative of your report? And are your plans for next year faithfully reflected in next year's targets?

Remember that for suspicious readers of your report (i.e. most of them), if you don't have and discuss KPIs and targets, for both past and future performance, that provide tangible evidence for the delivery of the main points of your strategy, then the report is window dressing.

> *The KPIs used in the analysis should be those that the directors judge are most effective in assessing progress against objectives or strategy.*
> FRC, Guidance on the Strategic Report (2018), p.35

On the governance and remuneration sections

This chapter has focused on storytelling because that's what companies are bad at, and on the strategic report in particular, because that's the section that does the bulk of the storytelling. It's also the crunchiest bit of the report: people go to the strategic report for the story, to the financials for the cold numbers, and to the remuneration section for the hot numbers (more on this below). The governance statement, for most readers, is a bit less interesting really. It remains, however, a major part of the report, and deserves a little attention here.

Governance has a story too
The first point to make is that all the above discussion about who reporting is for, the risks of window dressing, and the value of transparency, applies equally to the governance statement. The only thing to add is that storytelling does too; more perhaps than you'd have thought.

The key problem governance sections face is that they tend to get filled up with disclosures about policies and processes which, unfortunately, look a lot alike. Yes the Board meets quarterly, yes it makes use of reviewing mechanisms and dashboards, yes it has sub-committees on all the things it's supposed to... All this is well and good, but it's also all very boilerplate. Governance statements get widely criticised for precisely this quality, but then as companies protest, and not without reason, they're obliged to say something about all these things, and what are they supposed to do? They can't each invent corporate governance anew.

However, what the policies and processes by themselves don't tell us is the one thing that, from a storytelling perspective, we're most interested in: i.e. what our hero – which, in the case of the governance section, is the Board – has actually thought and done.

The Board as hero, seen in action
Setting aside everything on the governance section checklist,[1] the most important thing to cover is the Board in action. We need to see our hero doing stuff. The context should have been set already in the strategic report (it's the same business environment), and so what we want to know

---

1 Many governance checklist items can in fact be included as a checklist for those who need to see they're there. And many long-form policies, especially those that don't change from year to year, can be shipped to an appendix or, better still, a webpage, with just a link in the report. Much of the FRC's 'cut clutter' drive was focused on ensuring that standard items of this kind were not bulking up reports unnecessarily, and compromising comprehensibility with sheer unwieldiness.

now is how the Board is responding. What has been discussed at Board meetings? What are the principal decisions that have been made? How were they made, and in whose interests? What actions have been taken as a result, and what have been the outcomes? What as a company are you now doing differently because of the Board's decisions, and what, if anything, is the Board now doing differently, and why? And, of course, how does the Board in action connect up with the main story of the report?

This is the kind of information that too often is missing from governance sections, and its absence is what creates the boilerplate feel. All large companies have Boards and decision-making processes, but the actual decisions made by individual Boards are unique. These decisions, and how they play out, are in fact what make any one company *that* company, and not another.[1]

Remuneration as reward for action done well

The remuneration section is a little like the governance section in being somewhat bound by checklist requirements, and a lot like the financial statements in being considerably bound by accounting requirements, and the need to produce a series of specific numbers and supporting pieces of information. Having successfully complied with all these demands, the authors of remuneration sections typically feel tired, or at least reticent, and beat a retreat.

This however is a shame because, as discussed above (see 'Finding your beginning, middle and end'), ideally the logic of the remuneration section should flow out of the 'action + context' story, just as the strategy, KPIs, outcomes and purpose all should, and interconnect in a fluidly linked whole. Indeed the KPIs specifically should link directly and tangibly to the remuneration section, where they provide the final proof, in a sense, of the whole connective flow, by showing that directors are indeed paying themselves on their ability to deliver progress on their own chosen actions and strategy. In short, if a director believes that this action is the right thing to do, it makes sense that he or she should be paid for doing it well.

A lack of sense seems to be the main objection to remuneration sections at present. Readers tend to complain of opacity, and of not being

---

[1] The UK's recent reporting requirement for directors to include a statement on their compliance with section 172 of the Companies Act 2006 is the latest regulatory effort to address this issue.

able to work out how much ultimately the remuneration is, and what it's really for (or is contingent upon). In 2018-19, 9% of FTSE 350 companies linked all their KPIs to remuneration; 21% linked some; and the rest made no link at all. What were these executives getting paid for if not for delivering the strategy?

There is a trend among companies that want to be more transparent to include an 'at a glance' section, along with the Committee Chairman's letter, at the start of the remuneration report. However even these can be opaque, and subject to the same general criticisms (generic, evasive, incomplete, etc.) and risk of window dressing. Nevertheless, being less immediately bound by complex accounting requirements, these introductory texts are the place to lay out simply and clearly the connections and essential story that readers are looking for here: i.e. how what you're doing as a company, and how you're measuring it, feed into pay.

And a final point on wider stakeholders
When the report, with its story, is at last put in front of readers, the demands they have of it are fundamentally the same: they want the story to be coherent, accessible, and evidenced by relevant numbers. This is true for all of the three key reader groups – the shareholders, the company itself, and the wider stakeholders. But as the newest group within this trio, and the least well-recognised, it is worth asking: is the traditional company story, as set out above, enough for wider stakeholders?

On some level, yes. Stakeholders come to the report for a true, compelling and connected story just as much as anyone else, and won't be fobbed off with a little light community-washing. At the same time, and also like anyone else, they want to be able to see themselves in the story. In part, this means the report has to provide the rich contextual information that allows any reader to put him- or herself in the company's position, and think, *'Ah yes, if I were there...'* (as discussed above). But because the starting point of wider stakeholders is just that little bit less inside the company than shareholders and company directors, the report needs to work that little bit harder to help them feel 'in'.

Talking about stakeholders in the annual report
The most obvious thing reporting can do, and which it is doing already, is to say more about stakeholders in its treatment of the context.

A company that defines who its stakeholders are and how it engages with them is making a good start. But what's considerably better is to say something about what the stakeholders had to say back. Reporting, 'I talked to Neville,' is one thing, but, 'I talked to Neville and he said x,' proves I actually listened. And better still would be, 'I talked to Neville and he said x, and that's why I'm doing y.'

In a good example of the regulatory tail trying to wag the company dog, there is now a statutory requirement to include a section 172 statement in the strategic report, and it covers almost precisely this. Again as discussed above (see 'From shareholder to stakeholder'), large companies now have to say who their stakeholders are, how they engage with them, and what the effect has been on their decisions during the year. And to meet this requirement, we see companies now starting to include stakeholder tables in their reports, in which they line up, in rows: stakeholder groups; and in columns: engagement with those stakeholder groups, stakeholder responses, and company responses.

However sticking in a stakeholder table – perhaps even on p.167 – is not the sum of good stakeholder inclusion. As with everything, the information must connect with the story flowing throughout the report. To be a material aspect of the context, stakeholder concerns should be appropriately reflected in the strategy, and the strategic response should in turn feed into the KPIs and performance data. Indeed, as a further exercise along the lines of the 'connecting the flow' ones above, but for wider stakeholders, it would be possible to add two further columns to the stakeholder table, and use them to try to match company strategy and KPIs to the various stakeholder groups and what they had to say.

Companies and regulation are both already moving in this direction, and the coming years will see wider stakeholders getting more coverage in annual reports, and, hopefully, in a more connected way.

And including them too

What remains to add is one further thing that companies could do to make stakeholders feel more included in their reports, which is literally to include some. This isn't something that compliance will demand, but it is in line with the ongoing trend of reports becoming more people-y, and featuring more pictures and quotes – for example from senior leadership. To bring a little human interest to stakeholder disclosures, a similar move could be made with individual stakeholders.

Importantly, this does not mean just dropping in pictures of random employees from the company's photo database. Instead, to be meaningful, pictures of employees and/or other stakeholders should be accompanied by their names, and something from or about them. This could be a quote, or a little story, such that their inclusion becomes almost like a case study, or mini-magazine feature.[1]

The immediate risk is that this can look schmaltzy, and there is no doubt that companies can over-schmaltz in their efforts to appear stakeholder-friendly. A global finance company, for example, that covers its report with pictures of smiling kids from some tiny, one-off, local initiative, is frankly toe-curling. But at the same time, the mixing of large-scale contextual information with touches of *relevant* human interest can work very well, and indeed there is considerable precedent for this kind of mixing – for example, in the field of journalism (including that of the highest quality). A journalistic account of, say, an event involving thousands of people, will typically include crowd data and a few vox pops from individuals who were there. The vox pops are a meaningful addition to the account because they give human insight, and we as human readers respond to that information in a slightly different way.

Companies can draw on the same technique when talking about their thousands, or even millions, of wider stakeholders. By putting a few in your report, alongside their names and words, you show that you can relate to them as people. You also allow your readers to relate to them, and to their part of your overall story. Plus, after centuries of being neglected by reporting, stakeholders may feel that a little catch-up schmaltz wouldn't go amiss. After all, and as we know from Netflix, schmaltz sells. ∎

---

[1] Companies may worry that this could be logistically challenging as well as risky. Permissions will be needed, and what if the person moves on, or worse, is involved in a scandal of some kind? All true. It's certainly more work than just sticking in pictures of random stakeholders, but then it's precisely that work of engaging with individual stakeholders, and having confidence in the relationship with them, that makes the move to include them personally in the report so powerful. It effectively evidences some degree of communication and trust between a stakeholder and the corporate reporting machine. On the subject specifically of people (e.g. employees) moving on after being featured in this way, this needn't in fact be such a concern. An annual report is annual, and the expectation of readers is simply that that person was there, doing that thing, at that time. If they subsequently move on, they move on.

A!

To recap

Corporate reporting should be about telling the truth, and the trust that this engenders between companies and the world in which they operate. But telling the truth is hard. Both the history of reporting, and its fundamental dynamics, suggest that while the world always wants more truth, companies have a tendency at times to tell a little bit less. Writers of today's reports would do well to remember this when determining how 'aspirational' to be, as readers may view their efforts with a suspicious eye.

There is however a benefit to such scrutiny: it means you have people's attention. Use that attention well and your report becomes a valuable tool to communicate relevant information about your company to your shareholders, your stakeholders and, most importantly, to yourself.

But to communicate effectively, you need to tell a story. This doesn't mean making one up. Far from it, the basis of a company's story must always be what that company is doing – i.e. its actions – set in context, meaning the business environment in which it operates. The company strategy is simply the logic of how the actions respond to the context, and following them through points to the objectives, the KPIs, and the high-level purpose.

The key quality of this is how the information all connects and flows together. This makes the story easy to remember and, therefore, easy to tell. If it isn't, the reader won't get it. Their attention will drift, and with it, your chance.

Try closing your annual report, looking someone in the eye, and telling them the story. Start, 'This report is about...'

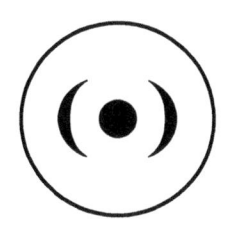

A lawyer's view

*A conversation with **Will Chalk**, former Partner and Head of Corporate Governance at international law firm, Addleshaw Goddard LLP (AG) and **Richard Preston**, Managing Associate and principal author of the Company Secretary's Checklist*

Q – Who reads annual reports?
A – Fifteen years ago, people were far less interested in how companies made money; investors were far more interested in how much they made. Today, while we don't think there has been a vast uptick in the numbers reading annual reports – after all, there are many other ways you can find information about a company – a greater range of stakeholders are reading them. For example, there is an increasingly inquisitive category of consumers, particularly Gen-X, while wider stakeholder interest has permeated the whole value chain. And, of course, this emphasis on stakeholders has been reflected in the latest regulatory requirements. Added to which, the revised Stewardship Code is driving more institutions to make their own decisions on governance practices as opposed to relying on proxy voting agencies to do it for them – and the foundation for those decisions is the annual report.

Q – Do they serve their purpose?
A – That's a difficult question. Their purpose is to build trust in business by informing investors' initial and ongoing decisions, and with a broader range of stakeholders through a responsible business agenda. Being accountable to all these different stakeholders means the annual report is trying to fulfil various purposes, and it's hard to achieve all that in one document.

However, the real benefit of good reporting is that the information it contains can – and should – set the foundation and tone of corporate communications for the rest of the year. Many companies have grasped that from a factual point of view, other departments – Investor Relations, Business Development – know that reports contain verified information which can be used elsewhere. However, there is an opportunity for companies to be much more strategic in the way that they use annual report information for other communications, but it means that reporting must be done well in the first place.

Q – You read many annual reports – what do they tell you about how UK plc views reporting?
A – It's quite telling that most companies – not all, but most – will take the legal compliance points we raise, and park most of the rest (the more qualitative suggestions about meeting the spirit of the regulations) for another time. That lays bare the fact that, for many, it's still viewed primarily as an exercise in compliance rather than communication. It's not surprising though – we've got to a point of too much regulation, too much compliance, such that many under-resourced reporting teams simply don't have the time to focus on anything other than ticking the boxes correctly.

> ❝ *The information a report contains should set the foundation and tone of corporate communications for the rest of the year.* ❞

Q – What would make annual reports more valuable and useful?
A – Only include what's material and relevant – a report does not need to cover everything in detail to be comprehensive. That, in turn, will allow an annual report to be clear and engaging to its readers. But how to determine what is relevant? It's about understanding why you're being asked to disclose something. We see plenty of things that are totally immaterial, and it tends to be because, quite understandably, companies use last year's annual report as their starting point. People therefore don't know why something is in the draft, assume it must be there for some regulatory purpose, and are scared to take it out.

Q – How could reports be written better?
A – Regulation is mainly to blame here. Coherence is clearly a vitally important ingredient. However, with different bodies having had jurisdiction over different parts of the report at different times, we've ended up with layers of regulation and overlapping requirements seeking to achieve the same end but in different ways. And, if you simply write by following the list of requirements for each section, you will get repetition and confusion. So you need to take a step back before you start, really plan what you're going to write, and how it all fits together.

In principle that's easy – but you need to have one person in overall control, who understands why things should be reported, and can co-ordinate contributions, edit them and push back to contributors. In practice, for many, that's not the reality, because most companies don't have such an individual. Many annual reports we read look like they've been drafted by five or six different people with no one taking overall ownership. The worst reports reflect an internal organisational situation where you have bits of the report that are personal fiefdoms of certain teams and are off limits for others to change – even when they know they need to be changed! This leads to the right disclosures in the wrong place, and even conflicting disclosures… and a lot of repetition. An annual report can therefore be very telling about the internal realities of a company, which in itself may not be a message you want to give to readers. So, that overall control is worth aiming for, however hard fought it may be.

Having said that, where there are individual voices – committee chairs, for example – they should be involved in writing their own reports. The best reports, that actually talk about what a committee has been doing and thinking during the year and why, stand out a mile.

Q – How could companies make preparing the report easier for their teams?

A – The annual report is a massively time-consuming project. Reporting teams are pushed for time and resources, so their starting point is what they did last year, rather than a fresh approach. 'As long as it's not wrong' is the main problem, because by 'wrong' people mean counter to the letter rather than the spirit of regulation. As we know, producing an annual report, certainly for some sectors, has moved way beyond just being an exercise in compliance. Senior leadership needs to understand that and provide the time, resource and backing for their reporting teams to meet these new expectations, as well as giving an overall editor a proper mandate.

❝ *There's no reason why certain information shouldn't be published on a company's website, rather than in the annual report.* ❞

Q – And what could the regulators do?
A – From a legislative point of view, the sheer volume of disclosure is the main issue. It seems that the easiest way for public policy to influence business is by forcing companies to disclose something, usually in the annual report. And so every consultation seems to end up with some kind of legislative change that requires you to add more! This undermines the readability of the entire document, because these disclosures may well not fit within a company's overall story, and so they just sit there, usually in the hinterland of the Directors' Report, alongside a number of other disclosures which seem to add absolutely nothing.

Legislators should think harder about this – there's no reason why certain information shouldn't be published on a company's website, rather than in the annual report. The Modern Slavery Statement is a good example. After all, it's about getting information into the hands of shareholders and stakeholders, and in some cases, directly on the website may be the best means of doing so. Legislators should act in a more joined-up way to avoid overlapping and conflicting requirements.

But there is hope – the FRC's Future of Corporate Reporting Project is looking at a revised model for reporting. In truth, it's not the first time the issue has been addressed, but there is probably more appetite for change today than there's been for a long time, so there is some cause for optimism! ■

Addleshaw Goddard's Corporate Governance team advises listed companies on governance and compliance, and other aspects of reporting.

Q – And what could the regulators do?
A – From a legislative point of view, the sheer volume of disclosure is the main issue. It seems that the easiest way for public policy to influence business is by forcing companies to disclose something, usually in the annual report. And so every consultation seems to end up with some kind of legislative change that requires you to add more! This undermines the readability of the entire document, because these disclosures may well not fit within a company's overall story, and so they just sit there, usually in the hinterland of the Directors' Report, alongside a number of other disclosures which seem to add absolutely nothing.

Legislators should think harder about this – there's no reason why certain information shouldn't be published on a company's website, rather than in the annual report. The Modern Slavery Statement is a good example. After all, it's about getting information into the hands of shareholders and stakeholders, and in some cases, directly on the website may be the best means of doing so. Legislators should act in a more joined-up way to avoid overlapping and conflicting requirements.

But there is hope – the FRC's Future of Corporate Reporting Project is looking at a revised model for reporting. In truth, it's not the first time the issue has been addressed, but there is probably more appetite for change today than there's been for a long time, so there is some cause for optimism! ∎

Addleshaw Goddard's Corporate Governance team advises listed companies on governance and compliance, and other aspects of reporting.

CHAPTER 2

In or out?

What else reporting's about (and may be about soon)

by Claire Bodanis

Q?

Questions this chapter will answer

- What else are people reporting on?
- What other reporting frameworks are there?
- Why do I need to know about them?
- What is ESG reporting and how important is it?
- Should I report against the UN SDGs?
- What should I know about where reporting's going?

P ART OF OUR BRIEF FOR THIS BOOK was that it shouldn't date – or at least, not too quickly. That's quite difficult for a book about reporting, given how busy the government and regulatory bodies have been in the last couple of years – and still are. And, of course, given the upsurge in stakeholder interest in all matters corporate, particularly around climate change and good (or bad) corporate behaviour. So I fully expect (and hope, actually) that this chapter's discussion on what else you might be reporting on, and where reporting is going, will be factually out of date by the time it's published, because some of the things it talks about will have moved into the annual report itself and therefore into the scope of Chapter 1.

But, while some of the facts may have moved on, the discussion will still be pertinent to what you're doing now. Not least because the ultimate test of whether or not something should go into your annual report now is whether you consider it to be relevant (or 'material', to use the reporting term) and therefore of importance to your shareholders and wider stakeholders.

Why is reporting always changing?
Reporting is determined by the purpose of business. In simplistic terms, when that purpose was only to provide a return to shareholders, reporting's reason for being was relatively straightforward too – report financial performance and the company's stewardship of investors' money (see the history of reporting section in Chapter 1, page 22).

Almost from the time investment began, however, there has been a debate about the role of business in our world beyond investor returns. In recent years it's hotted up as global companies have grown bigger and therefore more powerful even than some small countries, and concern over their influence has increased. It's particularly pertinent today in the immediate context of how the role of business in society may change in the aftermath of Covid-19, and in the wider context of climate change and the very future of our planet. Increasingly, companies are no longer being viewed as existing solely, or even necessarily principally,[1] to be good stewards of investors' money.

One of the latest UK reporting requirements is that directors must include a statement on their compliance with section 172 of the Companies Act 2006,[2] namely how they have promoted the success of the company for shareholders and having regard to its stakeholders – employees, suppliers, customers, the community and the environment. Another recent development in UK reporting regulation in this vein is the requirement for a company to report on its own unique purpose beyond making money. Of course, many companies have been founded on and continue to exist for just such a purpose – think of all the chocolate companies that were founded by Quakers to provide an alternative to alcohol, perceived at the time as a social evil. Unfortunately, the requirement to report on a purpose beyond money has resulted in a slew of utterly banal and empty corporate statements, but, let's hope, will ultimately serve a more valuable end.

In the USA, the Business Roundtable, an association of CEOs of America's largest companies, issued a statement in 2019 redefining the purpose of companies and committing to deliver value to all stakeholders. In the UK, the British Academy's ongoing Future of the Corporation project has determined eight 'Principles for Purposeful Business' which aim to 'provide a robust and positive framework to reshape business with the purpose and resilience required to contribute solutions as crises unfold'. And, in January 2020, the World Economic Forum's

---

[1] Some people forget that, unless the capitalist model of a company fundamentally changes, profitability and liquidity are essential for a company's survival. A company that doesn't end up making money (whatever it chooses to do with it) will cease to exist and will therefore have no impact, positive or negative, on anything else.

[2] Why companies have to report on compliance with something that's a requirement anyway is one of the bugbears I have with reporting regulation, which doesn't trust the reader to judge for him- or herself whether or not a company has complied with a requirement, and so asks the company both to do it and to say they've done it. It's hardly conducive to the concise reporting that regulators also say they are looking for.

International Business Council launched a consultation on how to report sustainable value, based on the notion that 'society is best served by corporations that have aligned their goals to the long-term goals of society' (more on that below). As the purpose of business is reframed, therefore, the role of the annual report also has to change to ensure it continues to reflect that purpose.

Whose interests matter most?

So far, so logical. But, while it's relatively straightforward to agree measures of performance that will show what a company has done with its investors' money, it's a lot harder to determine, let alone agree, how a company has looked after the rather more varied and fluid concept of stakeholders' interests. Or, indeed, how those interests and impacts could be expressed in financial terms, either positive or negative. The latest development in UK reporting is the requirement to report against the Task Force on Climate-related Financial Disclosures, whose aim is to get companies to assess the potential financial impact – positive or negative – on their business resulting from climate change. By doing so, the theory goes, investors will have a better understanding of the risks and opportunities of their investment. And, by virtue of that exercise, the narrative around it should also give other stakeholders a better understanding of the company's position on climate change, and what, if anything, it's really doing about it.

But which stakeholders? Which interests? If a stakeholder says he or she has an interest, is that enough to mean a company should pay attention? And what about the environment? Or the planet? That's considered a stakeholder all by itself now. Who speaks for the planet? Who has the authority to do so? Says who? Why? There are some interests which most people who have a voice in this debate agree are important – usually things companies shouldn't do rather than things they should, such as banning child labour from their supply chains in countries where it is still legal. Even that is a complex question, because the exercise of such bans could end up meaning children are exploited more, are forced to work under the radar, and get paid even less, if the structures aren't in place to ensure that instead of working they're going to school, which is the point of the ban in the first place. Again, more questions and more complexity. On these issues there isn't just one answer, let alone just one question.

From consensus to reporting

Reporting follows consensus. As subjects like the importance of carbon emissions in global warming become mainstream, companies are required to report on them, a shift from 'report if it's material to your business', to 'we know it's material so you need to report it'. But of course things that aren't common to all businesses are never as clear cut as things that are (like what happens to money – although even that's never all that clear cut), and some things are more relevant to some businesses than others. This is why, in the UK at least, the basic tenet of reporting is that, aside from the things that are obviously relevant to all companies, you as a company should decide what is material to you and report on that. The readers can then judge for themselves whether or not you've gone far enough, and whether they believe what you're saying.

When it comes to reporting, the further a company's interests (or responsibilities, depending on your point of view) lie outside things in its immediate control, or that are easily analysed, measured and reported on, the more scope there has to be for thoughtfulness, interpretation and an individual approach based on a company's own unique circumstances.

> **HOW DO I DETERMINE WHAT'S 'MATERIAL' AND SO SHOULD GO IN THE ANNUAL REPORT?**
>
> Materiality is about knowing your own business inside out. It's therefore a Board and senior leadership discussion. Too many 'materiality analyses' happen further down in companies, often carried out by those interested in wider stakeholders, but don't make their way up to the top, and thus don't bear any true relation to the real strategy and direction of the business. This is clearly an issue when it comes to determining if a report is fair, balanced and understandable (FBU), because if the proper analysis has not been done, one can have no confidence that it is indeed FBU. See Chapter 1's story approach for more on how to think about what's material and should be included in the annual report, and for a discussion of FBU.

The value of principles over rules

For this reason I'm a great believer in the UK's principles-based approach to reporting, so very different from the rules-based approach favoured by the US (see dual listings case study on pages 151-153 for more on that). It's far more revealing to explain why you've chosen a framework, or certain indicators, or how you've interpreted and enacted a principle, than it is simply to report against a list of pre-determined criteria, particularly if not all criteria apply to you anyway. It's also far more meaningful to your readers and more inclusive, assuming, that is, that the readers want to know what's really going on, rather than just compare consistent stats between companies and hope for the best.

A general reader should be able to understand a UK annual report if it's done well; I defy any general reader (or even some specialist readers) to understand a Form 20F, the US equivalent for non-US-domiciled companies listed in the US. Because of their format, 20Fs are virtually unreadable – even though, to be fair, some companies do try to make the information under the proscribed headings as accessible as possible. But that's the point. A 20F is there to comply with a list of rules, and you can go and look things up in it if you want. But to look things up you need to know what you're looking for – so you have to have pre-knowledge to use a 20F easily. Hence the specialist. And the real understanding of how each of those facts relates to each other is also left to the mind of the reader. The UK system requires the company to do that thinking itself, and present its story to the reader, which is a more fundamentally testing, exposing exercise than filling in a form.

Non-financial reporting frameworks and why they matter
This need for thoughtfulness is why I'm a fan of the plethora of reporting frameworks – IIRC, GRI, UNGC, TCFD, SASB (see box on pages 74-75) and so forth – which all come at non-financial reporting from their own angle. It's also why I am wary of complete standardisation for things that are not truly measurable in numbers alone and aren't consistent for everyone (more on that below). Non-financial information and indicators are a case in point. As frustrated company secretaries who get marked down unfairly by environmental, social and governance (ESG) ratings agencies will know, there isn't a single set of indicators that applies equally to every company, and some indicators simply aren't relevant to everyone.

To bring this back to the annual report, why is it important to know about non-financial frameworks, if you're only responsible for the annual report?

Are you sure you know all your risks?
First, from the perspective of relevance. You are required to report on social and environmental factors that *you consider to be material* – i.e. that create either an opportunity or a risk to your business that you should therefore be telling people about (particularly on the risk side). You need to have a really good handle on who your stakeholders are, what your impacts are, what you think is and isn't your responsibility to manage, and if others might quibble with that analysis. If you don't, it could come back to bite you in a very big way if something goes wrong. (See Chapter 6 on how communications, particularly social media, can be both friend and foe in those scenarios.)

You – and your risk team and senior leadership – should have this all sewn up for the short term, and possibly even the medium term. What non-financial reporting is really about, though, is trying to determine likely value in the longer term. It's about things that might happen, sometime in the future, which could have a big impact on you, either for the better or for the worse. And so it requires scenario thinking or, in plain English, imagination.

Imagination – a Board-level discussion
It can be very hard to imagine what might affect your business, particularly if you're not an imaginative person and are trying to conjure it up out of thin air (although really you shouldn't be doing this on your own – it should be a Board/senior leadership discussion). These non-financial frameworks are therefore useful for giving a sense of what other people are thinking about, the kinds of things they have imagined as possible risks or opportunities, and so can be used as a spur to your own thinking. This is where knowing what your competitors or peers are doing with regards non-statutory reporting is also useful – because if they're reporting on something that you're not, it might be a risk, or indeed an opportunity, that you haven't thought of. The story approach set out in Chapter 1 can help here – and is where, of course, reporting and strategic thinking overlap. Ideally reporting wouldn't drive strategic thinking, because senior leadership are so aware of what's going on that they're thinking about it anyway, but it can be a very useful prod if not enough of that thinking is being done.

Do you really know what's being reported everywhere?
Second, there's a practical point too. As the owner of the annual report, you should be aware of everything your company is reporting, whether or not it is within the requirements of this year's annual report, so you can ensure consistency across all your corporate communications. There may be non-financial reporting happening outside the annual report, or other required disclosure, that you don't know about. This might sound a bit patronising if you work in a small company – of course you're going to know. But when it comes to large, global companies, with many corporate functions, divisions, regions, and subsidiaries, and many thousands of employees, it's all too easy to miss what's going on elsewhere. For example, a local sustainability team decides to produce a report on a set of indicators, without reference to Group, who discovers it quite by accident – something I have seen more than once.

There are also the Group sustainability teams, who, frustrated by a lack of progress in changing corporate behaviour internally, quietly get a sustainability report out unheralded, by recruiting a sympathetic exec team member to sign off certain commitments to measure impacts and gather data. Commitments which have to be honoured because they're in the public domain, and, of course, have been signed off in the report by the Chairman or the CEO, who probably only read their intro and had no idea what they were committing themselves to. Again, something I've seen more than once – and, a case of the reporting tail usefully wagging the company dog, as discussed in Chapter 1.

> **DON'T FORGET THE MANDATORY DISCLOSURES OUTSIDE THE ANNUAL REPORT...**
> Companies are required to disclose many things that fall outside the scope of the annual report – notable recent ones being your position on modern slavery or on gender pay. Make sure you're aware of everything you have to disclose, not least because, if any of these are a real issue for you, they would, by virtue of their relevance, fall into the 'materiality' bucket, and should feature in the annual report anyway.

So – whether it's just because you should know what's going on, or because you want to take an active part in shaping your company's strategic direction, knowing about these frameworks (and that there are many others as well) is useful, if not essential.

SOME OF THE MOST COMMON NON-FINANCIAL REPORTING FRAMEWORKS

Here are some of the common ones used by global companies; there may also be other specific frameworks for your sector. And, there are other indices that rate companies based on non-financial metrics, such as CDP, FTSE4Good and the DJSI 'family' (now part of a wider group of indices), which it would help to be aware of.

Task Force on Climate-related Financial Disclosures (TCFD)

Chaired by Michael Bloomberg, TCFD was set up to quantify climate risk in terms of its potential financial impact on a company, and to include that in the annual report. Companies are asked to make disclosures that cover their governance and strategy around climate change risk, and how they are managing that risk, plus relevant metrics and targets. The original aim was that companies would take this on voluntarily, and many did, but it is now mandatory for premium-listed companies in the UK with financial years starting on or after 1 January 2021.

Value Reporting Foundation (VRF)

In June 2021, the IIRC and SASB merged to form the global not-for-profit VRF, to help simplify a common approach to value creation and reporting. Their respective integrated reporting frameworks and industry-specific sustainability accounting standards remain useful resources for non-financial reporting, and for demonstrating the underlying connectivity of sustainability performance with financial reporting.

International Integrated Reporting Council

The IIRC was a global coalition of regulators, investors, companies, standard setters, the accounting profession and NGOs who felt that corporate reporting should be properly 'integrated' and talk about many forms of value, not just financial. In 2013 they launched a principles-based reporting framework, founded on how a company interacts with the external environment and six 'capitals' to create value for investors and other significant stakeholders. These capitals are: financial, manufactured, human, intellectual, social/relationship and natural.

Sustainability Accounting Standards Board (SASB)

SASB was founded in the US in 2011 to develop a set of accounting standards that aim to quantify as far as possible in financial terms the impact of sustainability – meaning environmental, social and governance topics. Its aim is to 'connect businesses and investors on the financial impacts of sustainability', by looking at non-financial information from the perspective of the investor. It therefore restricts itself to what can reasonably be argued as being material, and differentiates between sectors with different sustainability impacts.

Global Reporting Initiative (GRI)

GRI has been pioneering sustainability reporting since 1997. Its Sustainability Reporting Standards – which are free – are one of the most comprehensive set of sustainability indicators for the management and reporting of economic, environmental and social issues. Many companies use GRI to create an 'index' of non-financial information.

United Nations Global Compact (UNGC)

Reporting against UNGC requires a company to produce a 'Communication on Progress'. It has three minimum requirements: a statement by the CEO expressing support for UNGC; a description of practical actions describing what the company has done against ten principles; and a measurement of outcomes. The principles cover human rights, labour, environmental issues and anti-corruption.

United Nations Sustainable Development Goals (UN SDGs)

The SDGs, set in 2015 by the UN with a target date of 2030, are a collection of 17 global goals for economic, environmental and social issues designed to be a 'blueprint to achieve a better and more sustainable future for all'. They were a call to action for countries to act in global partnership, but business has recognised it has an important part to play. There is increasing expectation from stakeholders that companies will make reference to the SDGs in their reporting.

How important is ESG reporting to investors?

'ESG', or environmental, social and governance matters, is the latest catch-all term for non-financial information, and defines the information now considered necessary for measuring the sustainability and societal impact of a company. It's the most recent example of reporting following consensus – or it will be when a consistent approach to ESG reporting is adopted, as seems hopeful (more on this below). The idea that 'ESG' is somehow something brand new and exciting must, however, be quite frustrating to those who've been banging on about the importance of these issues for years, represented in the hitherto niche area of socially responsible investment (SRI). But, let's hope they take comfort from being right – because the reason SRI has gone mainstream as ESG, and has suddenly acquired the status it has in directors' minds, is because investors are asking questions about it, and thinking about making investment decisions as a result of the answers they're getting.

The years 2020 and 2021 saw an explosion of interest from the investment community in ESG, with barely a day going by without an ESG-related issue appearing in the business press, be it financial industry regulation, proposals for carbon taxes, green credit facilities, criticism of inflated executive pay and so on. This interest is no doubt because two global crises dominated the world and are likely to do so for some time to come: Covid-19 and the climate emergency. While there are many ESG issues at play in both of these, at heart Covid-19 is a social issue (which may have stemmed from an environmental one) and the climate emergency an environmental one. In this context, even cynics can no longer argue that ESG issues are a reputational add-on with no financial consequences.

Rather, managing ESG issues well has now been recognised by investors the world over as essential for medium- to long-term growth and financial performance. This can be seen in the massive increase of capital flowing into ESG investments and funds. In April 2021, the *Financial Times* reported that ESG funds had attracted around $340 billion in the past two years, 'almost twice as much as the rest of the stock fund universe combined'. Interest in ESG investing reached such a point that, in mid-2021, there was talk of an 'ESG bubble' – that ESG was just another old-fashioned bubble caused by overexcitement in the market about the latest trend. Many expressed concerns that too much focus on non-financial issues would end in tears, arguing that it came at the expense of the financial returns necessary for keeping investors happy and for companies to remain in business.

Given the vast investment required to achieve the carbon transition necessary for the world to save itself, however, talk of ESG bubbles seems a case of the ostrich with its head in the sand. But, behind the scepticism in some quarters of the race to invest in assets with strong ESG credentials, lies a genuine concern, which is central to the challenges of reporting on ESG issues. And that is: what actually constitutes an ESG fund? What should make a company eligible (or not) for inclusion in such a fund, and why? There is no single, agreed definition of either. Therefore, how can we entirely trust data that, for example, claims superior returns for ESG companies?

> ❝ *Managing ESG issues well has now been recognised by investors the world over as essential for medium- to long-term growth and financial performance.* ❞

What is an ESG stock to one investor may not be to another – and to the general public the inclusion of certain companies in self-named ESG funds may come as a surprise, because, to that public, 'ESG', if they've heard of it at all, is a kind of shorthand for 'good'. Amazon, for example, is included in some ESG funds, while in my view it should be on the 'sin stock' not the ESG list because of its appalling record on tax and poor working conditions, let alone its march towards monopoly of the retail space. Turning to the UK, another company included in many self-named ESG funds is fast-fashion company Boohoo. Aside from the question of whether fast fashion itself is compatible with ESG principles, Boohoo was rocked by scandal in summer 2020 for near sweatshop conditions in some of the UK factories in its supply chain. On the other side, global chemicals company Johnson Matthey, which is developing

SHOULD I INCLUDE THE UN SDGS IN THE ANNUAL REPORT?

The UN SDGs were launched in 2015, but they have recently gained traction, no doubt because their target date is 2030, and companies (as well as the governments they were targeted at) are realising that there's now less than a decade left to do anything. Plus, climate action (goal 13) has sped up the agenda. So everyone is talking about them. There is no requirement to report in any meaningful way on the SDGs, nor even to mention them at all, because they were designed for countries, not corporates – but there are two points to consider.

1. **If you don't mention them at all people will ask why** – because it's become an expectation that any properly run company will have a position on the SDGs.

2. **If you do mention them, make sure what you say is true and credible.** It's the same as any other aspect of reporting. If you've done nothing at all about the SDGs and they haven't been part of your thinking, then be honest and say so, and explain why. If you say something glib to pay lip service to the SDGs, it'll be glaringly obvious. If you do choose to adopt certain goals (and here I'm veering into strategic rather than reporting advice, but the boundary is fuzzy sometimes), make sure they are truly relevant to your business. Too many companies blithely talk about supporting all the goals, or pick off gender, for example, because it's a popular choice right now. In reporting on the SDGs, you should apply the same materiality test to them as you would to anything else: Can your company make a meaningful difference to that SDG that is worth reporting on?

sustainable technologies for transitioning to a low-carbon economy, is generally excluded from ESG funds because of a blanket view that 'chemicals' are somehow 'bad'. Clearly, then, any data on ESG funds and their performance should be scrutinised and treated with a certain amount of caution – at least until we have better information.

This adds another layer of complexity to the thorny issue of how to report well. A frequent complaint from companies is that, as a recent Black Sun study found, 'in the current rush to invest in ESG funds, large swathes of investments are channelled into passive exchange traded funds (ETFs) which often rely on a single third-party ESG rating provider as their sole ESG element because this is cost-effective and requires limited expertise. This is a frustrating direction of travel for corporates who may feel obliged to spend unacceptable amounts of time on ticking the boxes and following the agenda of raters and rankers who often focus on disclosure and policies over tangible measures of performance'. Or worse, raters and rankers just get it wrong, as one FTSE Company Secretary complained: 'We got a negative ESG rating because the ratings agency had missed our disclosure of certain data, but when we tried to get it corrected, the answer was effectively "computer says no".'

There is now widespread agreement that non-financial as well as financial reporting is essential for judging whether a company or a fund is worth investing in. But without some kind of consistent approach to ESG reporting, it is difficult for companies to report well, and thus for investors to make well-informed judgements.

The future of reporting – a consistent approach to ESG
This information problem, combined with the acceptance of the importance of non-financial information spurred by the increasing urgency of tackling climate change, lies behind the growing calls from the investment community, listed companies and others for standardisation of ESG reporting, and as much consistency as possible in the metrics used. And the good news is that it has engendered a tremendous push from the business community – companies, auditors, standard setters, regulators – to make change happen fast.

In January 2020, the World Economic Forum International Business Council (WEF IBC), in partnership with the big four audit firms, launched a consultation at Davos with the laudable aim of standardising ESG reporting or measuring 'stakeholder capitalism'. While the resulting framework and set of metrics launched in 2021 is by no means the ultimate solution – as acknowledged by IBC Chairman Brian Moynihan, who reflected that WEF and the big four 'obviously aren't in the standard-setting business' – it was a useful exercise in engaging the corporate community. And, no doubt, it also helped speed up action from regulators and standard-setting bodies on both sides of the Atlantic throughout 2020 and 2021.

In the US, the regulatory body the Securities and Exchange Commission (SEC) has finally got on board with the need to report on non-financial issues, particularly climate change, while in Europe, the EU has already introduced new legislation in the form of the Corporate Sustainability Reporting Directive (CSRD), due to come into force in 2023. The CSRD builds on the EU's Non-Financial Reporting Directive, or NFRD, and EU Taxonomy (a classification system to determine what economic activities can be considered 'green'). It is far more comprehensive about the information companies must report than the NFRD, while making such disclosure mandatory.

> *As the climate crisis becomes ever more urgent, and with it the calls for better ESG reporting, it is likely that, once established, the ISSB will move quickly, although the issues it will have to grapple with in setting consistent reporting standards are complex indeed.*

The potential of the IFRS Foundation's International Sustainability Standards Board

But perhaps the most exciting development in the reporting standards landscape comes from the International Financial Reporting Standards (IFRS) Foundation, which is proposing a new, collaborative International Sustainability Standards Board (ISSB). Building on existing frameworks like GRI, SASB and TCFD, the ISSB aims to set global non-financial reporting standards, operating alongside the existing International Accounting Standards Board which sets the IFRS standards.

Why exciting? While progress in different jurisdictions is important, the holy grail for reporters and stakeholders alike is a consistent, *global* approach. And opinion seems to be coalescing around the ISSB – from the investment community, in the form of a growing number of pension funds and institutional investors; from existing non-financial reporting bodies; and even from WEF IBC and the big four, who have acknowledged that the IFRS may be best placed to create a set of standards, offering their own work as a preliminary list of topics and metrics for consideration. Perhaps more significantly, though, the ISSB has the backing of various governments including the UK (although the EU, perhaps because it already has the CSRD in train, has yet to indicate its position), while the SEC has signalled support, and it has received the blessing of the international Financial Stability Board, and the International Organisation of Securities Commissions.

The ISSB is due to be formally launched by the time of the UN climate change summit (COP26) in November 2021. As the climate crisis becomes ever more urgent, and with it the calls for better ESG reporting, it is likely that, once established, the ISSB will move quickly, although the issues it will have to grapple with in setting consistent reporting standards are complex indeed.

The ability to determine what genuinely constitutes 'good performance' against ESG issues, to hold companies to account and compare one with another is without question a good thing. But there is a danger inherent in the push to standardisation, namely the idea – which is espoused by some – that a single set of disclosure boxes to tick will solve the problem. It can't. When it comes to non-financial reporting, much depends on context – even more so, perhaps than with financial reporting. What is significant for one industry may not be to another, while even within the same industry, what is significant for one company may not be even for a direct competitor. And, of course, different stakeholders have different views on what they believe matters most.

Nonetheless, a useful, consistent *approach* is not impossible, and I believe the ISSB has a good chance of success. This is because the IFRS has, to date, proved its usefulness as a set of financial reporting standards, and in doing so, hasn't done away with the narrative, principles-based reporting approach I so favour in the UK. It has resisted the temptation to take the superficially easy, but dangerous, box-ticking approach to reporting that is anathema to good communication and erodes trust. There is good cause for hope, then, that any non-financial standards proposed by the same body would walk that careful – but so essential – line between a mandated list of disclosures and the flexibility of the narrative 'comply or explain' approach. Any dilution of the UK's requirement for directors to determine what is material to the business and report on that – namely, to tell their story truthfully – would be a catastrophe for reporting, and by extension for business and society.

The communication challenge – too long, or not long enough?
Where does all this leave the annual report and those who have to produce it? First, it is essential to stay on top of changes in reporting requirements and legislation because things are moving so fast. Simply remaining compliant is a challenge in itself. But, going back to the purpose of reporting – excellent communication that builds trust with stakeholders – the bigger challenge at hand is that the push to include ever more ESG information in the annual report is increasing the tension between communication and disclosure. Or, as Chapter 1 puts it, telling stories and ticking boxes.

Because of their length, and the difficulty of working out how to produce a document that does both, many annual reports have become virtually unreadable. So they are neither serving their purpose of telling the company's story for those who want to read it, nor of providing a list of information that knowledgeable folk can easily look up. But there is general consensus that this state of affairs cannot continue. While information is power, and companies have a duty to be transparent with investors and other stakeholders, there comes a point where the burden of regulation clouds a company's unique and important story. And, it can also be easier for the unscrupulous to hide in the undergrowth: the increase in reporting regulation has not stopped unexpected corporate failures and has perhaps even contributed to the further erosion of people's trust in business.

Recognising this, there have been many projects and reviews recently looking at the future of reporting. None so far has really achieved much in the way of tackling this problem, and there don't appear to be any bold proposals in the pipeline. However, with audit reform and the standardisation of ESG reporting requirements on their way, without question the annual report will evolve yet again. So it's more important than ever that those with a stake in it get involved in shaping this evolution so that future changes enhance rather than hinder the purpose of reporting.

And let's not be despondent. Despite all these challenges, and all this change in the offing, good reporting *does* exist. It *is* possible to cut through the noise, to report well, and build trust with stakeholders through reporting. After all, that's what this book is all about. ■

> ❝ *It is essential to stay on top of changes in reporting requirements and legislation because things are moving so fast.* ❞

A PLEA FROM PRACTITIONER TO REGULATOR...

In the meantime, until this new dawn arrives, a plea from a practitioner to the regulators: please consider a) the fundamental purpose of reporting which is to engender trust between business and stakeholders, and b) what the practical consequences are of a regulation, which may actually go counter to that purpose. The problem with most new regulation is that it doesn't appear to consider part b) at all – as the recent palaver around the introduction of the European Single Electronic Format (ESEF) illustrates (see case study part 1 on page 86).

Instead, it appears to come from the position of 'we want companies to do *x* so we'll get them to put it in the annual report, and then the auditors will make sure they've done it', or perhaps 'this would be good for investors, so we'll get the report to do it'. That may be because not enough practitioners are consulted – or perhaps they're just too busy to take part in any consultations because of all the work they have to do in producing their annual report! Whatever the reasons, a much better conversation between practitioners and regulators could only be a good thing for reporting – and for the trust so essential for a harmonious society.

A!

Useful things to know about non-statutory reporting
- Know your non-financial information – even non-statutory requirements may be necessary for the annual report because they fall into the scope of what's relevant ('material') to your business
- Deciding what non-financial information is material for reporting should be a Board and senior leadership discussion – because it's about the true value and health of your business
- Non-financial reporting frameworks can be helpful in prompting ideas of what might be material
- And they're an indicator of what's coming from new regulation
- Other parts of your business may be reporting things you're not aware of – so make sure you find out

Where reporting's going and why
- Reporting reflects the purpose of business – so as that purpose changes, so too does reporting
- Non-financial (ESG) reporting is becoming mainstream, because investors are interested and the stakes are getting higher, particularly on environmental issues
- Standardisation of non-financial reporting is a popular endeavour, but will only work if narrative reporting with its comply or explain principle is retained alongside standardisation of metrics
- Get involved with the development of reporting regulation as much as you can – respond on behalf of your company to consultations, and make your voice heard

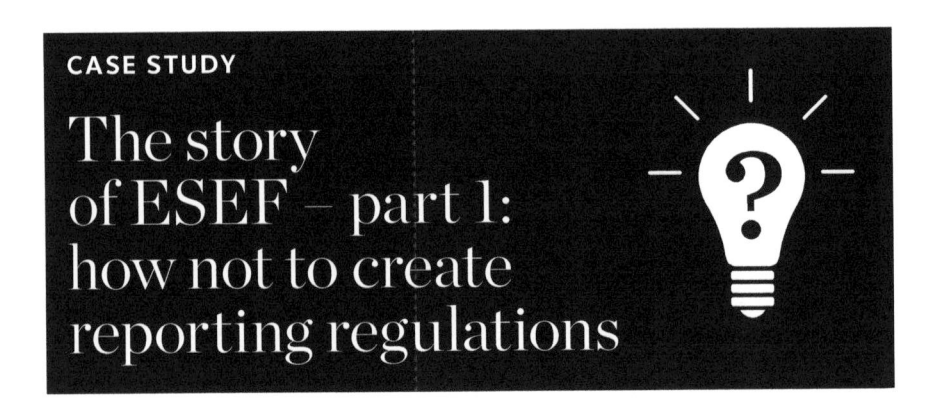

CASE STUDY

The story of ESEF – part 1: how not to create reporting regulations

The story of ESEF is a classic tale of how a misguided regulation has added greatly to the burden of companies to little practical effect – as part 1 explains. But, as we find in part 2, it's also a tale of how such things can have positive consequences, thanks to the ingenuity of technological experts. Prompted by the constraints of regulation, they are using the potential of digital to reimagine reporting for all channels and all audiences, both human and machine.

PART 1: HOW NOT TO CREATE REPORTING REGULATIONS

The latest development in annual report production is the requirement for companies across Europe (and it still applies to UK companies despite Brexit) to produce the ESEF – the European Single Electronic Format. This means companies must file their annual reports as tagged XHTML documents (to enable their readability by machine readers), and the regulation came into force for reporting periods beginning on or after 1 January 2021 (delayed from 2020 as a result of the pandemic). It's the practical consequence of the EU Transparency Directive, that 'requires issuers listed on regulated markets to prepare their annual financial reports (AFR) in an ESEF', and was developed by ESMA, the European Securities and Markets Authority, at the behest of the EU.

The story of ESEF is a perfect example of poor regulation, namely of how a really good idea – the laudable aim of facilitating 'accessibility, analysis and comparability of annual financial reports' – founders in practice because the practical reality and the consequences of its implementation have not been considered in the making of the regulation. In this case, those making the rules had not properly thought about a) who reads annual reports and why, and b) how reports are actually produced.

What exactly do you have to do to file an ESEF?

There are two things that are different from the current PDF filing format. One, tagging of certain data (which will be familiar to those responsible for filing to HMRC for tax purposes, and those filing reports in the US); and two, the preparation of the annual report as an XHTML document. For the first two years the financial statements will need to be tagged in the XBRL taggable format, with the whole annual report filed as an XHTML document, and from 2023, the notes to the accounts will also need to be tagged. While there is no suggestion (yet) of tagging the strategic and governance reports, it hasn't been ruled out. I hope it will though, because while data is consistent between companies, how each company interprets reporting regulations and tells its own story through narrative reporting is unique – or should be – and is therefore not comparable through tagging.

What's the purpose of the ESEF?

Which brings me to the purpose of the ESEF, which is to make it much easier for investors to compare reports with each other. This is a great aim. And, when it comes to data that is the same between companies, a technological solution of tagging which means you can use a machine reader to extract the data you want from lots of reports at once, and spit it out in a format that compares it for you, makes perfect sense. So the tagging element of ESEF is very sensible – although the lack of provision for such a machine reader, or a central repository for housing all these new reports, does blow a huge hole in the practical usability of the new format (more on that below).

What doesn't make any sense at all is the requirement to publish the full annual report as XHTML, or the suggestion that narrative reporting might be tagged. It is unclear what purpose filing the whole annual report in XHTML will serve – except as the (unnecessary) vehicle for holding the tagged financial statements. With regards to tagging narrative reporting, it's a nonsense because, as this book explains, the whole essence of good narrative reporting is that it is unique. Tagging requires a taxonomy that is consistent across the system so that the machine reader can read it and extract the information. This is entirely contrary to the UK's principles-based narrative reporting approach. So tagging in relation to strategic and governance reports would serve no purpose – what, in fact, would you tag?

This point was very well made by the FRC in their January 2016 response to ESMA's original consultation about which electronic format should be chosen: 'We believe it is important to consider the application to structured and unstructured data separately. We consider iXBRL as being the best-suited technology for structured information. We believe that PDF represents the current best option for unstructured data.'

How will people be able to access and use ESEF reports?

When I first heard about the new regulation, I assumed that the regulatory authorities would be creating a central repository in which all the thousands of reports filed in this new format across the EU would live, along with some kind of portal and machine reader to do the reading, thus opening up reporting for anyone wishing to look at and work with these public documents. But there is no such portal or repository, and, as far as I understand it, only the beginnings of a plan by the EU to create one.

Professional investors and companies are already well served by companies like Bloomberg which take each company's financial statements as soon as they're published, tag them and make the data available through their platform and, quite reasonably, charge for this service. So, unless people either subscribe to one of these services, or create their own software and their own system and database for picking up and storing every EU- or UK-listed report, then these machine-readable documents will languish un-machine-read and unused by their intended audience. And, the regulation simply means that companies will have to pay for the work of doing the tagging that Bloomberg and their ilk are already doing as part of their service.

For this regulation to be truly useful for those other than institutional investors and corporates who already have the benefit of tagged documents, then a central repository must be created. The problem with creating one, however, lies in the fact that currently companies file their reports in their own national reporting repository (in the case of the UK, the National Storage Mechanism). And a pan-European one, while now in the planning stages, may still be a long time in coming - no doubt long after companies have been required to produce the ESEF.

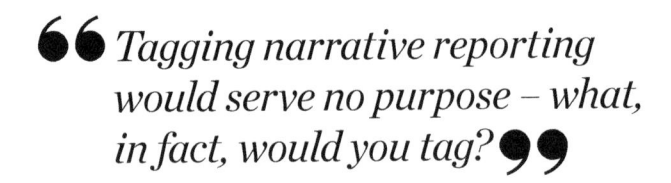

> ❝ *Tagging narrative reporting would serve no purpose – what, in fact, would you tag?* ❞

Why was this format chosen if very few people will, in practice, be able to use it?

ESMA ran a consultation in 2015-16 on how the regulation should be implemented. As already quoted above, the FRC very sensibly recommended that the tagging of financial statements be done in XBRL and kept separate from the annual report that should remain a PDF. However, the vast majority of respondents recommended the XBRL/XHTML solution. Why is this?

At the risk of sounding like *Private Eye*, if you look into the responses, a pretty depressing story emerges. The consultation went out to around 7,000 companies and bodies across the EU. ESMA received about 80 (eighty – this is not a typo) responses, around one quarter of which came from technology companies that sold XBRL/XHTML solutions. Why ESMA didn't listen to a knowledgeable body like the FRC instead of technology companies who clearly had a vested interest in the outcome is anyone's guess. But at the very least ESMA is guilty of laziness – a consultation that gets a response rate of barely 1% should not be the basis for a sweeping change.

Apparently ESMA also held discussions with various Board directors, who thought that this single format sounded like a good idea. But, as we know, while the principle is a good one, it's in the implementation that the problem lies. Board directors are some of the least well-informed people within a company to comment on the practical implications of producing annual reports, since they rarely get heavily involved; and ESMA clearly did little if any research with the implementors. If they had, the practical issues we're discussing here would have surfaced and, one hopes, resulted in a better outcome.

What does the ESEF mean in practice for producing the annual report?

When this regulation was first announced, there was a huge amount of consternation around its implications, because at the time, the creation of a tagged XHTML version was a totally different process from how we usually write and design the standard PDF version of the annual report. And, at the time, there was no way of turning the PDF into XHTML. It seemed we were looking at either having to create separate documents to enable the PDF version to continue for human readers, or that the PDF would disappear and an undesigned, Word document-type approach that could be created in XHTML would replace it, thus making reports largely inaccessible to human readers.

Fortunately, in late 2019, technology solved this problem and PDFs can now be converted into XHTML, with the necessary data tagged. The process of tagging, largely the province of companies' finance departments who are accustomed to doing this for other filing requirements, is not entirely straightforward, however, and companies would be well advised to do a practice run on their latest published report. At the time of writing, only a few early adopters had published ESEFs in the UK (although more in Europe had done so), and the results are best described as mixed, with many reports containing errors in tagging and formatting. But with luck, these will prove to be teething problems that will sort themselves out as people get used to producing the ESEF.

Overall, however, what the ESEF regulation leaves us with in practical terms is an additional burden on the already stretched annual report process, and an additional cost for companies to pay for tagging and XHTML conversion (how much remains to be seen). And for what benefit?

> **Those making the regulations and those carrying them out must work together to improve reporting for everyone.**

Who will benefit from the ESEF?

Until the EU creates a central repository and machine reader service for ESEF annual reports that enables them to be accessed by all, then the only real beneficiaries of this new regulation are those who charge for their services in producing them. And possibly Bloomberg and others who will no longer have to do the tagging themselves, because companies will have done it already. There is no benefit to the companies themselves, and little benefit to investors, because those professionals most likely to have the resources to access the machine-readable versions are already served.

What can we learn from the ESEF experience?

On the positive side, reporting regulation could be really useful in promoting positive change. The idea behind ESEF – that much of the data inside annual reports is comparable and should be much more readily available to be analysed and compared by investors and others seeking to use it – is a great one. But, if the implications are not thought through properly, then the implementation of a new reporting regulation can just add cost and complexity for no discernible benefit. Which brings me back to the central theme of this book which is that we need to keep in our minds at all times what reporting is for, and why we are doing things, to make sure that what we are doing will continue to serve reporting's purpose. And regulators need to do this just as much as everyone else.

Technology is massively important in enabling progress, but it is not an end in itself; it has to be aligned to reporting's purpose. There's a certain irony in the fact that technology has rescued the human readability of annual reports from its potential destruction by ESEF, through creating the PDF to XHTML conversion tool.

The biggest lesson? We need to work together. Those making the regulations and those having to carry them out must talk to each other and work in a constructive way to improve reporting for everyone. Otherwise regulation just gets a bad name, and that benefits no one. ∎

Postscript

Since this case study was written in 2020, developments on the tech front have given us cause to be hopeful that, from a poorly conceived, impractical requirement, may come great things for reporting... read on for part 2!

CASE STUDY

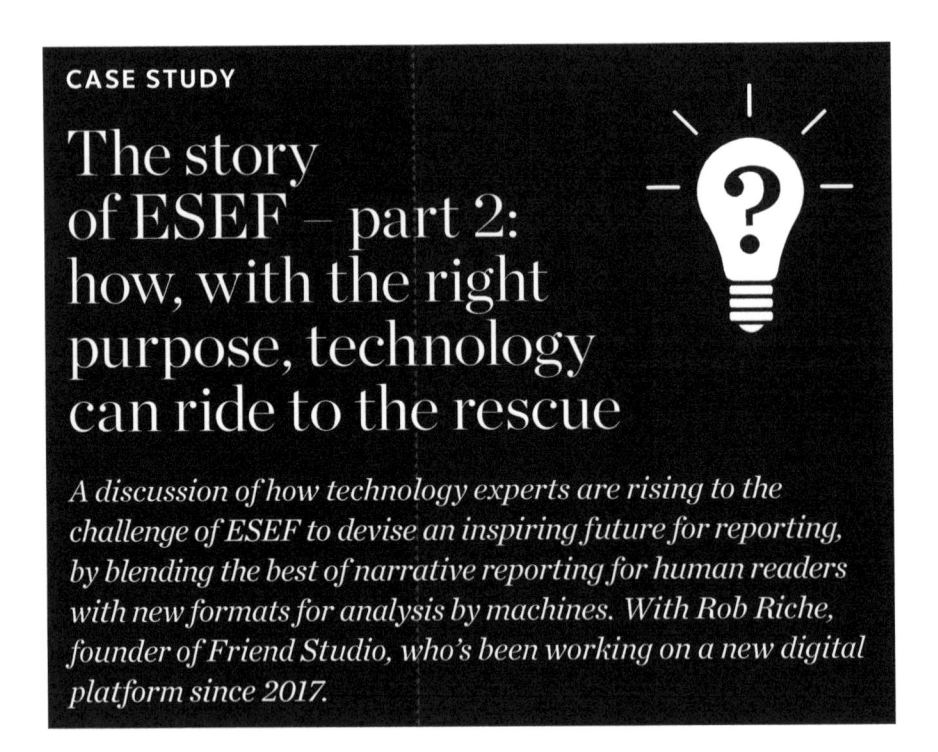

The story of ESEF – part 2: how, with the right purpose, technology can ride to the rescue

A discussion of how technology experts are rising to the challenge of ESEF to devise an inspiring future for reporting, by blending the best of narrative reporting for human readers with new formats for analysis by machines. With Rob Riche, founder of Friend Studio, who's been working on a new digital platform since 2017.

Why has reporting lagged behind other forms of communication in going digital?

In short, the technology to produce digital-led reports that meet *all* needs hasn't been viable – partly because the complex mix of content required today is challenging to create and deliver with digital publishing tools. As a result, most online reporting has, so far, been limited to summaries which accompany the PDF download. And, perhaps unsurprisingly, regulation has tended to focus more on content than on format.

But this is changing. As discussed in part 1, content regulations are now accompanied by new format requirements which will result in a more digital-led reporting model over the next few years. The iXBRL/HTML digital report (rather than the PDF) is now mandatory in all major markets. Driven by this, new software for publishing digital reports is already emerging which will take us beyond PDF functionality without losing its benefits, enabling a faster shift to digital.

It's important to note, however, that the best solutions don't start with technology, they start with a need. For the new world of data-enabled reporting to succeed, going digital will be about serving up the experience people want in a better way. Think of how digital has changed shopping, music or film – you're still getting the same content or product, but in a digitally-enabled way. And digital – when it works – doesn't replace everything that existed before. It keeps all the best bits and reshapes them. At Friend, we are already starting to shape new reporting technology to meet *all* stakeholders' needs.

Why do some people have concerns about the ESEF requirement?

As part 1 of this case study outlines, ESEF is an example of how regulation has hit on a good idea – comparable, data-led information – without considering how it will affect *all* uses of reporting, and without communicating its purpose or benefits. Most people we talk to don't even know why ESEF has been introduced, and certainly don't have time to wade through all the debates about where it came from and where it will lead.

Most information about ESEF has focused on the technical, financial and tagging requirements – understandable since they are complex. But presenting ESEF as *only* about XBRL tagging misses the biggest potential of this format: the opportunities and benefits it offers stakeholders and companies in terms of engagement, something we are doing our best to communicate.

People have been talking about 'digital-first reporting' for years – is there really a new dawn?

Having seen the full capabilities of the new ESEF format, we think so. But the focus shouldn't only be on the iXBRL requirement. The ESEF is essentially an HTML format, and this offers many opportunities for companies to transform how their reporting engages audiences digitally.

Anticipating the full effect of this potential is difficult today. But if you look at the history of digital technology, when something better becomes available, people will want it. And 'better' means giving people an experience they want or need.

There is an inevitability to reporting becoming more digital, and the ESEF requirements have given us the spur to embrace that. Despite all the technical complexity of ESEF, we are still bringing it back to the core purpose of reporting – engendering trust, through clear communication.

Although the current focus of digitisation is on the drier, financial and technical aspects of the new regulation, our attention is also on ESEF's powerful engagement capabilities, and its potential to transform digital report publishing. It is a revelation to discover that the ESEF has the capability to do anything digitally that a website can do – all that's missing are the tools to deliver it. We're now working hard on that, shaping technology so digital reports can be produced more efficiently, and meet the need of all audiences as well as the regulatory requirements.

To ensure we build tools that can deliver a future-ready reporting model, we've mapped out future stakeholder needs and regulations from what we already know. For example, we know that iXBRL and HTML are the foundation of all future digital reporting. We know that content isn't likely to shrink – it could be more concise but the requirement to disclose is only going to expand. We know that digital users demand direct-to-content searching (not big PDFs from a Google search). They also expect essentials like interactivity, responsiveness and video. And, we know that digital trust and accessibility is a really crucial issue for regulators, so robust audit, assurance and hosting will be essential.

We are now creating a new reporting model to meet all these needs, using digital tools that make it easier, more efficient and more automated for companies.

What does your vision of a digital future mean for the narrative report?

The fear many people have is that, in the relentless pursuit of digital, the purpose of reporting – engendering trust – for which narrative reporting is essential, will be forgotten. This fear is not unfounded, given what happened in the US with the SEC's implementation of XBRL, which appeared to ignore the value of communications to stakeholders. While XBRL is a brilliant vehicle for data-sharing and analysis at scale, in the raw content format required for filing to the SEC, it's pretty awful for most readers, who aren't data analysts. As a result, SEC reporting seems to have become a compliance information dump, with untrusted tagging that undermines the content, and is useful to only a tiny fraction of stakeholders. Worse still, it has made crucial assured and Board-signed communications and content inaccessible, potentially creating further mistrust of business.

> ❝ *The narrative flow that's at the heart of the best reporting can be completely retained in the digital space.* ❞

A few years ago, we saw signs of this influencing UK reporting, with some dual-listed companies' reports becoming little better than a tidy Word document, with poor design and content flow, and very little to inspire any reader. We believe the future of digital-led reporting doesn't need to be this way. It can retain all the best aspects of current reporting which have been shaped over many years around users' needs. And, as I explained already, we think the ESEF rules are better conceived than the SEC version of XBRL, with greater potential to have a positive effect on future reporting for *all* stakeholders.

It's worth stressing again, regardless of new delivery formats, that reporters must still prioritise the way their story is told. Even an innovative new format needs content that is valuable to audiences.

So, when can we expect to see reporting going fully digital?

We think it'll be a transitional process, starting with ESEF. Further progress will be driven by three main things: audiences' needs, more regulatory demands and new software (not widely in use yet). And it won't be a one-off change. As technology advances, we expect the workflows, report formats and regulations to evolve together.

At Friend, the heart of our vision is a purpose-built digital reporting platform – a content management system, developed by reporting and digital technology specialists, with new functions to meet the unique demands of reporting. To make the transition to digital seamless, it integrates with existing tools, and enables content editing, design, proofing, iXBRL tagging, digital publishing and filing all in one system. It means companies can publish *instantly* from a single source of content to *all* reporting formats, for *all* audiences – PDF, print, iXBRL and full digital reporting online. It also makes full digital reporting more cost-effective than ever.

This approach offers our clients a simple step into digital-first reporting, without needing to learn new software. The system is compatible with print-led design tools (PDF, CtrlPrint and InDesign) which makes full digital reporting easier to create.

So, alongside the immediate ESEF demands, we are also starting to prepare our clients for the longer-term, technology-enabled future that is coming to reporting, and we are happy to share our work on this with others.

Any advice for preparing the ESEF in the short term?

Using a specialist XBRL provider to convert and tag your PDF report is currently the simplest approach, and probably will be for a few years. It allows you to keep the print-led readable version while meeting the legal requirement to file an ESEF. It also means minimal changes to your existing reporting processes (just adding an extra stage). Not all tagging providers will suit all needs, but your agency should be able to let you know the options, and help you identify what will work best for you.

Starting early is our next tip. The taxonomy mapping and tagging prep can be done at any time, so don't leave it till you're in draft accounts stage. And, of course, having set it up well in the first year should make it easier in future years. Finally, don't assume ESEF is a static financial and compliance requirement. If you are involved in reporting, in any capacity, be ready to embrace further changes as ESEF sparks a revolution in the way we prepare, produce and deliver digital reporting over the coming years. Good luck! ■

CASE STUDY

Get involved and influence the future of reporting

A look inside the FRC's Future of Corporate Reporting Project and its outcomes with Thomas Toomse-Smith from the project team.

What's the background to the project?

It's a reflection of several things that have gone on around corporate reporting. Recent failures have driven the public and political mood to increasing concern over the crisis of trust between business and its stakeholders. We've seen the Kingman Review into our role as regulator; the Competition and Markets Authority Review of the audit sector; the Brydon Review into the quality and effectiveness of audit; and, more recently, the BEIS proposals for reform which synthesised recommendations from the earlier three. All these will have implications for the annual report in some way, but there hasn't been much discussion of the report itself, whether it's fit for purpose, and how we might change it if not. So we felt it was time to bring everyone's ideas together and look at the whole annual report, given its essential role in building trust in business.

> *Is the annual report in its current form doing a successful job, and if not, what should we do about it?*

What questions did you ask about reporting?

There's a lot of pressure on the annual report because of increasing regulation and guidance (and we hold our hands up here!). It's getting bigger and bigger to accommodate more and more information, and yet it has to serve lots of different stakeholders. So we asked questions like: who's really interested in the annual report and why? What information are people looking for? How could they best access that information? And, the ultimate question: is the annual report in its current form doing a successful job, and if not, what should we do about it?

What did you find out about what people are looking for in reporting?

As we found from our initial research, it depends who you talk to. But there were some surprises – including that interest wasn't based on the type of relationship people have with a company (e.g. an investor) but what they individually are interested in. For example, the investors aren't all just looking for IFRS disclosure, but have many different focuses.

The biggest surprise was actually how wide the interest in reporting is. As part of our research we spoke to the general public through a 'Citizens' Jury' project which, through panels held in London, Edinburgh and Coventry, asked a representative sample about their view of reporting, corporate governance and audit. Most people didn't know much about reporting, or had only a vague idea it existed, but as soon as they started thinking about what they'd like to know about companies, they quickly came to see value in reporting.

Were there any general themes?

You have to step away from the idea that specific stakeholders all want the same specific bits of information – actually people are looking for something quite wide. But the common theme was a need for informative reporting. There's a general interest in what a company's purpose is, and how it is achieving that purpose, which does somewhat conflict with the other thing people want, namely some basis of consistency to compare companies across the market. The same challenge we have at the moment, of course.

From the initial research, we came up with a model for what reporting might look like in the future, and ran a further consultation which drew responses from the business community. The model itself was based on the idea of a kind of digital CMS (content management system) for corporate reporting, that pushes the annual report boundary further than today. This 'reporting network' wasn't a single document, but a series of interconnected documents and disclosures joined together by a logical structure – which includes a mandatory business report bringing together elements of the strategic report with environmental, social and governance (ESG) disclosures. The idea was to offer more flexibility to ensure that the essential story piece didn't get clouded with lots of detail, while also allowing people to find the detail that they want.

We did, however, recognise the need to maintain the boundary of what's assured or audited and what isn't, while recognising that anything we proposed would have to be flexible enough to accommodate the upcoming changes in the audit space.

What did you conclude about reporting's future?

The idea of the model was to push the discussion forward, rather than coming to any specific conclusions now about a new way of reporting. What we heard in the responses to the model was that people widely accept the fact that other stakeholders are an important audience alongside shareholders, and that ESG issues clearly matter, although the area is changing fast with discussion around the development of a new global set of reporting standards. There was also an acceptance that technology needs to work harder for reporting.

What can reporters expect to see?

There isn't going to be a wholesale new annual report model any time soon. Rather, we're looking at different aspects of reporting to respond to the themes we heard during the various consultation stages of the project. For example, we will be taking steps to encourage high-quality ESG reporting, and we will be doing more work on how to make the most of digitisation.

What should reporters do now?

The key question for us is: what does the market think? We're therefore urging everyone involved in reporting to contribute to the next wave of consultations coming out not just from the FRC but from other bodies like the new Sustainability Standards Board set up by the IFRS Foundation. We believe that effective regulation strikes a balance between reflecting what leaders are already doing, and encouraging laggards to do more. So it's really important that people take part such that any regulation we propose will ultimately be beneficial, and the changes that result will achieve their purpose of reporting truly becoming a means of building trust with stakeholders. ■

> *We will be taking steps to encourage high-quality ESG reporting.*

CASE STUDY

Auditors should be thinkers, not bean counters

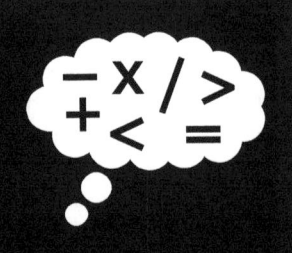

A discussion of the Brydon Review – an independent review by Sir Donald Brydon into the quality and effectiveness of audit – with investment and governance expert Paul Lee, who represented the investor community on the five-person Brydon secretariat, and who ensured that the voices of investors were heard throughout the process. Recommendations from the Review are being considered as part of the UK Government's proposals for audit reform.

KEY CHANGES PROPOSED BY THE BRYDON REVIEW

A new purpose for audit: 'to help establish and maintain deserved confidence in a company, in its directors and in the information for which they have responsibility to report, including the financial statements.'

- Audit to act in the interests of, and be useful to, all stakeholders, not just shareholders
- Establishment of audit as a proper profession in its own right – no longer an offshoot of accountancy
- Auditors should be thinkers who judge what they find by putting it into its broader context, and who act to inform others about their conclusions
- Suspicion to be celebrated as a key quality for an auditor
- Audit to go beyond financial statements
- A direct relationship between shareholders and auditors.

In or out?

The Review starts with two words – 'Language matters'. Why is this so central?

What lies at the heart of this Review – and chimes neatly with the theme of this book! – is the need for auditors to play a key role in building trust with stakeholders. To do this, audit needs to be far more informative to its users, those users being all stakeholders. And to be informative, auditors need to abandon deliberately professionalised language with its closed-door set of terms that mean nothing to anyone except insiders. Auditors need to get back to the natural meaning of words that everyone can understand. This is a fundamental shift in the thinking of what audit is for – namely to provide information to help all stakeholders understand a company and be able to trust what they read.

So what's audit for, if not to tick off the balance sheet?

Audit has always been about checking whether what a company says is true. But there's a huge difference between confirming that a figure on a balance sheet is an accurate number that's popped out of a robust financial system, and offering an opinion as to whether or not the figures presented really tell the story of what's going on. In fact, the Review finishes with an amusing poem which demonstrates very clearly what the issues are! The Review's proposed changes are trying to tackle this very problem, so that audit does indeed help stakeholders get a clear view of the whole story, not just of a few numbers.

THE ACCOUNTANT'S REPORT

Taken from the last page of the Brydon Review: said to originate from the 1930s, this poem demonstrates how many of the same criticisms have been levelled against audit for more than 80 years:

We have audited the balance sheet and here is our report:
The cash is overstated, the cashier being short;
The customers' receivables are very much past due,
If there are any good ones there are very, very few;

The inventories are out of date and practically junk,
And the method of their pricing is very largely bunk;
According to our figures the enterprise is wrecked…

But subject to these comments, the balance sheet's correct.

What does the new purpose mean for what auditors will actually do?

It's a big change. Auditors will need to have far more inquiring, in fact suspicious minds, and really delve into the inner workings of the company. They'll need to ask far more questions, challenge more, seek additional information – so that they can in all honesty give a company a clean bill of health. And, if they can't give a clean bill of health, they'll have to say so.

Won't companies be a bit wary of baring their souls to their auditors?

It depends how you look at it. Companies that want to commit fraud, hide things, mislead their shareholders and stakeholders – they certainly won't welcome this far more investigative approach. But, if we give companies the benefit of the doubt and assume that what they say in their annual reports is true, namely that they want to manage their risks well, that they want to know where they are falling short of their principles, that they want to be open and transparent with stakeholders – then they should welcome these new, investigative auditors. After all, in big companies in particular, the directors can't be everywhere and know everything. The new audit profession could become a very useful source of truth for directors – and they'll get much more value from the audit process than ever before if auditors are encouraged to seek out original information to inform their opinion.

And let's not forget, in today's world of instant communications, nothing's a secret for long. Isn't it better to find out some bad news from your auditor so you can manage the issue yourself, rather than read it for the first time on someone else's social media feed and have a PR crisis to deal with on top of everything else?

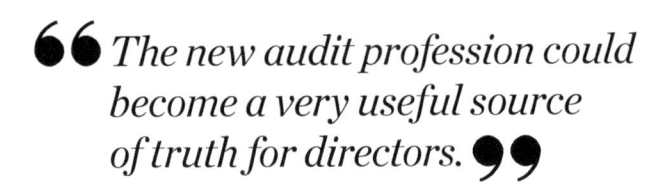

> ❝ *The new audit profession could become a very useful source of truth for directors.* ❞

Isn't this new audit process going to cost a lot and take much longer, maybe even delaying the results?

It is certainly likely to cost a bit more, but investors have already indicated that they'd be happy to see audit fees go up. And, to my previous point, if your investment in audit means you know more about your risks, it may save money in the long run. The process itself is certainly more in-depth, since it will cover more information in a more investigative way, and so may take longer – although auditors should also be involved much earlier in the thinking around reporting too.

But this is where I part company from those who say that annual results and reports should be published as soon as possible after the year end. This kind of pressure does not help shareholders, because if anything it means that information is compiled and audited with less rigour, and is therefore more prone to inaccuracy and so is less useful. We're all trying to make capitalism more long-termist – think ESG reporting – so why this obsession with getting the results out so early?

Assuming the proposals go through, what does it mean for reporting?

On a practical level, the Review mentions two changes for reporting – one, to replace the going concern (short-term) and viability (medium-term) statements with a single resilience statement. This will require directors to think about and report on the short, the medium and the long term; it's actually quite far-reaching because it'll mean a change in the way directors think about things – capital allocation, for example. And two, directors will need to make a public interest statement which sets out how the business is operating in the public interest. This takes the concept of reporting on company purpose to a whole new level since it means a stated purpose really needs substance behind it.

Aside from these practical considerations, though, the implications for reporting are much broader, and more beneficial to stakeholders. Audit is there to check whether what companies are saying is true. If their remit extends beyond confirming that certain financial boxes have been ticked correctly, to confirming whether the story presented is also correct, then reporting becomes a far more reliable source of a company's truth. ■

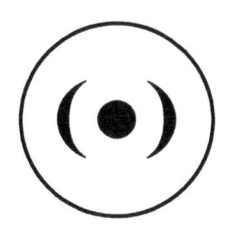

An investor's view 2

A conversation with **Sacha Sadan**, *former Director of Investment Stewardship at Legal & General Investment Management.*

Q – Are annual reports useful?
A – In today's focus on wider stakeholders, we mustn't forget that the primary purpose of the annual report is to look after shareholders' interests by holding companies to account. The annual report is principally a statement to shareholders of how they are doing. It is a document of record; historic, in the public domain, a place where the company cannot hide. A good annual report should be the starting point for understanding a company.

Q – What makes a good annual report?
A – It needs to be well written, with substance, and with thought for the reader. What does the reader want to know? How best can you get that message across, through words and visuals? It worries me when I see too much PR in an annual report, or if I read a Chairman's statement, for example, and it's clear he or she didn't write it because it really doesn't tell me anything. And reports must be focused and talk about the stuff that matters, rather than including everything which renders the whole meaningless.

Q – What do you look for in an annual report?
A – First of all – honesty. Reports should be written from the heart. It's in companies' interests to do that, because otherwise you will get found out, and investors will use it against you. Companies sometimes forget that their readers have memories – for example, if you had a big acquisition three years ago that hasn't gone so well, it's far more convincing to discuss that openly and explain how you'll do better next time, than brush it under the carpet. And investors will give you credit for that.

I'm also looking for evidence. Reports should discuss impact and outcomes, and have proper evidence and examples to back up their statements. A favourite for companies today is 'employees are our most important asset'. Fine – but where's the proof, for example, that you're paying the living wage? Why is the pay ratio between employees and the CEO so high if you really care about them? And, I'm particularly interested in what the Board is thinking about. I don't want to read about every single risk a company might conceivably face, just like any other company – I want to know what the directors are talking about in the boardroom. And I expect a tone of humility. All companies have issues to deal with; they need to discuss how they are working out what to do. That's what makes a report believable, and what gives me confidence that the Board and management are credible.

Today, I'm also increasingly looking for consideration of the longer term. Companies need to be paying attention to environmental, social and governance matters. A company cannot be a good long-term investment without that, and we are very much interested in investment for the long term.

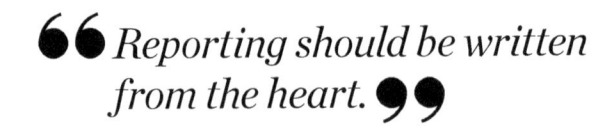

> ❝ *Reporting should be written from the heart.* ❞

Q – What's your view on the quality of reporting by UK plc?
A – It's certainly mixed. A lot of colleagues have given up on annual reports and look to the financial statements and other sources of information instead, because too many reports are full of empty words, and far too long. An annual report shouldn't be War and Peace! And, too often today, the top people outsource the thinking of the annual report when really it should be their primary concern. But the annual report remains the historic document of record, and increasingly contains more longer-term, forward-looking information that you don't get elsewhere. Annual reports, done well, written honestly, are very valuable in telling your story and proving yourselves to investors and, increasingly, other stakeholders. ■

Sacha heads up the Investment Stewardship team at LGIM, which champions responsible investment and good governance to protect the long-term interests of their clients and society as a whole. Sacha and his team are highly active in the consideration of environmental, social and governance (ESG) matters and their impact on the long-term value of LGIM's clients.

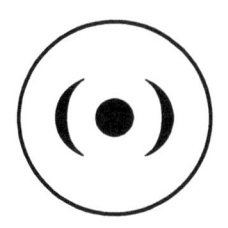

An auditor's view

A conversation with Maria Kepa, Director in EY's audit practice and UK Corporate Governance team.

Q – What is the value of reporting?
A – From a wider societal point of view, reporting has enormous value because requiring companies to report on something really focuses their attention and hopefully leads them to doing the right thing, which today includes consideration of a much wider group of stakeholders than just their shareholders. The gender pay gap requirement is one such example.

From an investment point of view, for me the most fundamental disclosure requirement is the business model. It brings real transparency to how a company makes money and delivers value to wider stakeholders. You can tell from good business model disclosure whether a company is responding to changing needs and trends in its context. Poor business model disclosure can be very telling.

Q – Do annual reports serve their purpose?
A – Annual reports are an important mechanism for companies to be able to communicate to their stakeholders. However, many people feel the reports are too long – they tend to build on what was included in previous years, rather than starting afresh – and a document that's unreadable doesn't create trust. Also, particularly in governance reporting, there is often far too much description of processes. How much trust do you feel in a company that talks about processes a committee has gone

through, but then doesn't tell you what the outcomes of those processes were? Some level of process description is needed so that we can judge the strength of their governance systems, but unless a process has fundamentally changed does it really have to be described in the annual report every year?

Q – Companies often complain that auditors make reporting unnecessarily difficult – what's your view?

A – There's always going to be a certain degree of tension between companies and their auditor, and so there should be – our role isn't to be liked but to be challenging and sceptical! We're there as objective outsiders to make sure that companies' reporting is materially accurate and fair so that it can be relied on by investors and wider stakeholders. It's true, though, that the process for everyone is getting harder.

There are more and more regulatory requirements that companies have to report on and auditors have to look at in the front half, but the time to do it isn't getting any longer. In fact, it's getting shorter in the drive for 'fast close' – i.e. to publish sooner. And it's not just a matter of throwing more people at it. As auditors, one of the things we're looking for is consistency between the front and the back half (as well as the knowledge obtained during the audit), and it's difficult to do that if different people are looking at each.

> ❝ *We need to balance the importance of greater disclosure with producing meaningful documents that people will actually read, and which will serve their proper purpose.* ❞

Q – Why is there such pressure to publish so quickly? Is it really necessary?

A – It comes from the time when reporting was really only about financials. Some people see early reporting as an affirmation of the strength of the financial close process – if you have robust processes then you can report quickly. But there's a growing tendency, which I agree with, to have numbers in the front half that don't come from the back half, i.e. the non-financial data. The processes behind those numbers tend to be less robust, and they are often harder to assure. And many people assume that all numbers are assured or audited, which of course they aren't. That being said, it's the Board's responsibility to oversee the accuracy of the numbers in the front half and consider the need for them to be assured. Arguably, the notion of a 'fast close' is becoming less essential given that much of the information isn't time-critical, and the information that is – the financial results – is published separately anyway.

Q – How could the reporting and auditing process be improved?

A – While positive progress is being made, some companies see reporting principally as a regulatory exercise rather than as an opportunity to build trust with their stakeholders. There is risk to approaching the annual report as a collection of tick boxes, allocating sections to different contributors instead of having a single author. This can sometimes lead to repetition as well as inconsistency. A report I read recently was at least 20 pages longer than it could have been because of this. Shorter, more coherent reports, containing only material information would, arguably, be easier to audit. But to be fair to companies, it's very difficult to do this, particularly when the default regulatory position seems to be to require more disclosure.

One of the key challenges lies in the quantity of information that reports have to contain now. Greater transparency is, of course, a good thing, because it can influence behaviour, but producing vast volumes of information can be counterproductive. Does everything that is currently required to be included in an annual report really have to be there? In the longer term, we need to balance the importance of greater disclosure with producing meaningful documents that people will actually read, and which will serve their proper purpose. Reporting is rendered meaningless if annual reports are on the one hand too long to be read and on the other, do not cater to the needs of stakeholders. There is also a real point of challenge – do many of the required disclosures have to go into the annual report rather than on a website or another portal? For example, much of what is in the strategic and governance reports is not, in fact, time-sensitive and could perhaps be published elsewhere at a different time of year.

However, disclosures in the annual report are perceived to be more externally visible and therefore receive greater internal scrutiny. So, for the foreseeable future I believe there is going to be a tension – on the one hand having a fair, balanced and understandable front half narrative; and on the other having to add more and more disclosures as a means of holding directors to account. That at least seems to me to be the likely trend, based on some of the proposals in the BEIS's white paper on audit reform. ■

> Maria is an experienced auditor of UK listed companies and specialises in corporate governance. She worked closely on the approach to corporate governance for the Embankment Project for Inclusive Capitalism (EPIC), which aims to promote a longer-term view of corporate value. Maria was also involved in the governance working group of the World Economic Forum's International Business Council.

CHAPTER 3

Fail to prepare, prepare to fail...

How to get the report done well, with minimum hassle and stress

by Kerry Watson

Q?

Questions this chapter will answer

- How and what should I prepare?
- Who should be involved?
- What's the role of senior leadership?
- How do I ensure people take it seriously when it's not their job?
- How do I manage so many people?
- How do I deal with changing regulations?
- How do I make sure the report is fair, balanced and understandable?
- How do I ensure the sign-off process goes smoothly?
- How do I make the best of remote working?

Fail to prepare, prepare to fail...

WHEN I STARTED MY CO SEC CAREER nearly 20 years ago, the annual reports we produced ran to about 70 pages. And getting it done in the time available seemed quite a challenge even then. In 2020, the average length of a FTSE 100 annual report was 185 pages, and some of the bigger ones, in the financial sector for example, ran to 300 plus. The work that goes into producing something this long, with no extra time, that complies with an ever-growing array of legal, governance and accounting standards, cannot be underestimated. And this is the bare minimum you have to achieve. Producing a beautifully designed, easy to read, investor-friendly report with a coherent story that will meet the ultimate objective of engendering trust with your stakeholders is even more difficult.

The challenges are numerous. Different contributors but the need to find a common voice; writing a coherent, informative, engaging story while including a plethora of legally required information that may or may not seem hugely relevant; keeping up with ever-changing legal and governance requirements; drawing together a disparate group of people to produce the largest and most important piece of communication with investors; and, from 2020, dealing with the challenges of virtual working (see special section on page 135).

But the opportunity is tremendous and worth the effort. The requirement to report can force Board conversations and clarity on the big issues – strategy, culture, risk, governance – which is good for the internal management of company operations, and good for communications with stakeholders. It can provide an insight into how the Board thinks and offer a useful benchmark when looking at the company as an investment proposition alongside your competitors and peers. It can create real engagement and constructive two-way dialogue with investors. And, given the requirement to tell the company story and cover subjects of interest to all your stakeholders, its content can – and should – form the foundation of how you communicate across all your channels. After all, the investment you have to make in producing the report is significant – why not use it to best effect? (More on this in Chapter 6.)

> **A TIP:**
> "A big benefit of reporting can be how it prompts a conversation about the big issues."
> FTSE 250 comms director, financial sector

So where and how to start? There are five key stages:
1. Define your purpose
2. Prepare absolutely everything
3. Plan your project in minute detail…
4. …and be ready to manage a changing process
5. Don't underestimate the approvals process.

With such a mammoth document, preparation and planning are the most important stages, and you need to give them a lot of time. It is never too early to start; in fact many large companies start planning their next annual report shortly after the publication of the last one.

1 Define your purpose

The ultimate purpose of the report should be to engender trust with your stakeholders – this is the guiding principle behind the regulations which require you to tell your story. And, if you're reading this book, you probably want to do reporting well. But I know from experience that, depending on your Board, sometimes it's just not possible to do anything more than produce a compliant document that satisfies the regulator. It's always worth fighting for doing the report well, but if ultimately that is the Board's direction, then you need to know, since it will determine what you do.

'Different Boards will have different approaches,' says a FTSE 100 company secretary from the energy sector. 'Some will just want to comply – a very low risk approach. Others will go beyond that and see the opportunity of talking to a wider range of stakeholders about the company's purpose. I don't think Boards are spending enough time talking about purpose – but it's useful to do it because it gets them thinking about the link to strategy.'

If you are looking to do reporting well, there may still be differences in approach, depending on the kind of company yours is. Do you work for a retail company that wants to appeal to consumers as well as investors? Or a newly listed company that needs primarily to get its investment proposition out there? And what has the company's performance been like? Company A, a mature company which has just had an *annus horribilis*, will obviously need a different tone and perhaps some different content to Company B, the disruptive new kid on the stock exchange.

Before starting any annual report, it's important to have clarity on what you want to achieve, who your primary internal stakeholders are and who you're writing it for. This may change over time, depending on the sector, maturity and performance of the company, so it's useful to revisit this every year. Of course, sometimes this is easier said than done – participants in the process may have different agendas – but if that's the case, at least agree on what balance is to be struck and how to achieve a good outcome for the competing priorities.

These objectives – and the story and messages that support them – will be central to the brief described in Chapter 4 (see pages 169-172) and guide the report's content and presentation.

2 Prepare absolutely everything

Detailed preparation in calmer times will make life much easier in the chaos of year end. The company secretary will usually be responsible for driving any changes in content that stem from regulatory and governance changes. He or she will necessarily own the governance section and may often be heavily involved in the drafting of the strategic report if familiar with boardroom conversations. Having this overview is a privileged position to be in, but it also means a heavy workload for the company secretary, and preparation ahead of time is key to making life a little easier.

Get the right reporting agency[1]

Assuming you're using an agency, getting the right one is essential. For a full discussion of how to work well with your agency (central to an easy process), including setting budgets, ways of working, choosing an agency, see Chapter 5 – but here are a few key points.

- Make sure you know what you want from your agency, so that you can find the right one with the right skills and expertise – and that includes setting a realistic budget.
- Working with a reporting agency that is responsive, right first time, challenging where necessary and on the same wavelength, will make the process much easier.
- If you're conducting a tender, look at agencies' previous work, take up references and make sure you meet the team, especially the project manager, the person you'll be working with most closely. In such a time-driven and pressurised environment, it makes an enormous difference to have someone you trust and can communicate with well.

A TIP:

"You want someone who listens carefully, takes the time to understand what you really want, and then works with you as a partner to deliver a high-quality end product."

FTSE 250 corporate relations director, food and beverage sector

---

1 See page 195 for a discussion of what a reporting agency is.

Review last year's report

Having laboured over the last annual report for months, and referred to it ad infinitum during the year, you would be forgiven for never wanting to look at it again. However, in the spirit of continuous improvement, it's always useful to review the report having had some distance from it, as well as reviewing any notes you may have made during or at the end of the process. Also, review any comments from last year's wash-up meeting with your agency, your auditor and the project team, along with your own notes from the year. What worked well and what didn't work so well?

And, don't forget to check with Investor Relations if there has there been any feedback from their meetings with investors during the year on what they would like to see.

> **A TIP:**
> "Keep a copy of the annual report on your desk throughout the year and scribble on it as things occur to you. Then you'll be ready for next year."
> FTSE 250 company secretary, property sector

And benchmark it against your peers

We all have the teacher's voice in our heads that says copying others is a bad thing. And they're right – copying what other companies do without considering whether it's right for you would be a bad thing to do, which is why we advise against the concept of 'best practice' as discussed in the introduction on page 6. But reviewing other annual reports is a good way to see where you are in the reporting pack, what other companies are doing and what could be borrowed and adapted to good effect for your own report.

You can also ask your agency – and perhaps even your auditors, although this is less common and is not part of the audit scope – to benchmark the previous year's report against peer companies – an external, objective view can be helpful. 'We ask our own auditors and designers to review the previous year and tell us what they think,' says a FTSE 250 company secretary. 'Even though as co sec I should know what's going on, it doesn't hurt to have a reminder! And we do carry out quite a lot of the recommendations.'

A number of corporate reporting awards with different emphases are published during the year, and it's natural to assume that the shortlisted and winning entries will be really good reports, worthy of selective adaptation. But beware: some awards are by submission (i.e. the company or agency sends in their own report) so there's a self-selecting element; and, as a recent awards judge told me, even those that aren't self-selecting don't necessarily result in a particularly good shortlist for the judges' consideration. So if you do look at award nominees, it should be with a significant degree of caution. In the end, knowing what works for communicating your company's ethos and staying true to that will work better than trying to copy 'best practice'(!).

Check for new requirements

As regulators busy themselves trying to make annual reports all things to all people, so the regulatory burden keeps increasing. While some new requirements are well-publicised and much talked about, there can be other minor technical regulations that need to be included. Bear in mind as well that compliance with some regulations will need to be well-thought out in advance, for example where the Board is required to report on how it has fulfilled a particular duty during the year. Otherwise you'll get to the end of the year and realise that you can't report on it because it hasn't been done!

Consider also whether any of your internal processes and sign-offs will need to change to accommodate new requirements.

⌐ Many law firms and accountancy firms run free seminars on changes in corporate reporting regulation which can be helpful in finding out what needs to be done. See also useful sources on pages 238-241. ⌐

Start with a blank sheet of paper

Being faced with a blank sheet of paper is daunting, as any company secretary will know from drafting Board papers and minutes. That's why it's so tempting to simply roll over last year's annual report and do a few quick updates. But if we do that, we're missing a big opportunity to challenge ourselves and our teams about what important issues to include and what we really want to get across to readers – i.e. we are not doing reporting well.

In an ideal world, the prior year's annual report would be used as source material rather than version one of the new report. But let's be realistic – the sheer volume of regulations and compliance requirements means that starting from scratch isn't always possible, particularly if you don't have much help in the team. Even if you can't do it completely though, it still helps to think about what you *would* write if faced with a blank sheet of paper. It can crystallise your thinking on themes, opportunities, potential pitfalls and what the reader really wants to know. Then you're in a position to make sure that the key points are included and come across clearly in the report – even if some of it is brought across from last year.

'Cut the clutter'

Cutting clutter in annual reports has been one of the FRC's objectives for a few years. It's something that's difficult to do and can go against our natural instinct – in the face of increasing regulation, and in the typically risk-averse mind of the company secretary, the safest approach is to add to rather than delete for fear of accidental non-compliance with a technical piece of legislation buried deep within the Companies Act. And lawyers, particularly US firms reviewing US-listed company reports, can be very reluctant for things to drop out from one year to the next, which doesn't help. But remember the ultimate purpose – for a report to be useful and meaningful, it must be readable, and simply adding more makes reports increasingly impenetrable. We need to help our readers out as much as possible. Chapter 4 explains how to make your report engaging and useful, but here are some key points:

- Review whether there is anything that can be deleted or edited
- Challenge whether there are areas that can be improved from last year. Are there things that would be better explained by a graphic, which would improve transparency and readability and cut down text?
- Is there any jargon that hinders the reader's understanding and could be explained in plain English?
- Is the annual report open and honest enough or does it fall into boilerplate disclosure? Does it give enough prominence to the right areas?

Get your leadership on board

How you engage with key internal stakeholders and get them on board with the reporting project will vary from company to company but it's crucial to the success of the annual report. Without buy-in from the top, it's difficult to make the annual report process anything other than a compliance exercise. If the Board and/or top executives take an interest, it suddenly becomes easier to manage roadblocks, engender a sense of pride in those working on it and ultimately produce a more meaningful report that gives a sense of what the company is about.

'The tone from the top really is important,' says a FTSE 100 retail sector company secretary. 'If the Board and CEO are engaged then it gets everyone else passionate about it too, while having Board comments on early drafts motivates others to behave in a good way.'

There should be buy-in from the top – after all, directors are responsible for approving the report, and therefore should be heavily involved right from the beginning. Unfortunately, this doesn't always happen, and many company secretaries have to deal with directors who have little interest in the report until they have to approve it. It's very difficult to get engagement from very busy people if they're not already committed, but here are some things that may help:
- Identify the key senior stakeholders and know their personalities: Who can offer support in pushing the annual report agenda? Who could be a potential roadblock, whether because of personality, lack of engagement or simply time pressure, and how could it best be dealt with?

- Get the CEO or CFO involved at the start of the process[1] – this can save a lot of re-work later on. And include your agency in that meeting, and anyone else involved in developing the brief. Even half an hour with the CEO and/or CFO will help prevent anything getting lost in translation. What have been the most important events in the year from the CEO's point of view? What does he/she want to highlight? Are you aiming for evolution from last year's report or is more change needed? If this meeting is unlikely to happen, try to find someone else at exec level who is party to discussions with the Board and investors who can provide that input instead.
- Senior stakeholders, especially divisional or business unit heads, often have different views, particularly when it comes to design. Be clear on who has the last say if there is dissent in the ranks.
- Tee up your approval process and make sure that all those involved – Board, auditors, lawyers, others – understand the purpose and what you're trying to achieve with the report. Things like tone, style and messaging are also important to explain, otherwise you may run into problems when they come to review it, having their own personal views of what a report should look like (see approval section below).

A TIP:

"Have conversations with the right people: if you're writing about the Board and strategy, it's daft to write it cold without having a conversation with those who are embedded in it all year."

FTSE 100 company secretary, utilities sector

---

[1] Many CEOs and CFOs, particularly of larger companies, aren't very interested in the annual report – but, for all the reasons discussed in this book, particularly Chapter 1, they should be! So it's worth making the effort.

3 Plan your project in minute detail...

Once you've finished the prep, you should now have a clear idea of the shape of the report, what needs to be included and what can be taken out or improved. Time for planning to begin.

With a process spanning months, it's important to have a really detailed plan that sets clear deadlines, explains the consequences of missing them, and that will raise flags if things go off track.

Set a detailed timetable

A detailed timetable is crucial for monitoring progress and making sure you will hit key dates. The timetable will vary from company to company but, generally, key dates should be aligned to relevant Board and Committee meetings, audit close meetings and any other internal sign-offs that are required. If you've done annual reports previously, you will have a timetable that will be rolled over from year to year, but it's always worth considering it in light of what worked well and what didn't work well in the prior year, and amending it as necessary. If key people change, the process may well need to change too, to accommodate them and their style of working. It's important to discuss the timetable with everyone involved so they understand what they need to do and when, and sign up to it.

Create a team...

See also the section on creating a team with your agency, Chapter 5, page 195.

There's no doubt that indirectly managing a large number of people and inputs across a range of functions is a challenge, particularly when many of those people will have a day job of their own with competing priorities, deadlines and managers. In larger companies, there is the additional challenge of working across different locations and silos. The annual report is a team effort and, as such, it's important to foster a team ethos for a normally disparate group of people.

A workshop at the start of the process can create that team spirit and instil a sense of pride in what you're about to create. It's important for ensuring everyone understands the annual report brief and process, gives them context on the corporate reporting environment and the value of the annual report, and, if you have internal people writing, helps them understand how their contribution fits into the whole. 'Our big kick-off workshop is very well received internally,' says a FTSE 100 retail sector company secretary. 'We make sure we set off on the right foot by agreeing tone, theme and messages.'

The workshop is also essential for getting everyone signed up to the schedule and plan: 'It helps everyone feel responsible for the annual report, and also helps with the process because people understand the impact on everyone else if they don't hit their deadlines.'

...and be clear about their responsibilities

'The annual report is a big job for three to five months of the year, so the project team needs a clear mandate from the Board and regular feedback loops,' says a FTSE 100 company secretary from the energy sector. This clear mandate is essential and will give you the authority to run the project. Beyond that:

- Agree on a **project co-ordinator**, and what his or her scope is. If you're using a reporting agency, this is usually the person who deals directly with them to avoid conflicting or confusing instructions.
- Agree who will be on the **working party** and make sure it's balanced – too few people and it could run into problems with resource or support, too many and it risks grinding the process to a halt. If possible, include a sympathetic senior stakeholder who can influence others if things start to go awry. In larger companies, you may have two working parties, a steering committee that includes the most senior decision-makers, and an operational committee that includes the doers.
- Agree **who is responsible for the 'common voice' or 'story'** of the annual report, ensuring that the front and back ends are married up and are fair, balanced and understandable. This may be the project co-ordinator, but it needn't be – the key requirement is that the person is a good writer and understands what should be said.

- If there are **different business units or business divisions** within the company, think hard about how you're going to involve them. They are usually best placed to give technical or marketing input, but will probably be less well-versed in drafting an annual report, and may find it difficult to set their information in the context of the overall company story. 'Make sure you have an editorial board with the authority to push back and reject content,' says a FTSE 100 company secretary. 'The business units need to allocate someone who is able to provide input on brief – and who is also prepared to be responsive to feedback. Parts of the business may want to use the report to pitch their own area, and the editorial board has to be able to step in to ensure consistency and balance.' Although do bear in mind that these contributors will have to verify the factual information, which is why ensuring you have a good relationship with them, and that they understand and buy into the big picture, is so important.
- Be clear on the responsibilities and **internal sign-offs** for each section of the report. A matrix can be helpful, setting out who is responsible for drafting, contributing, reviewing and approving each element. Comments should be sought only from the relevant people who can add value – too many inputs can slow down the process. But remember the dangers of leaving people out, as described by another retail sector company secretary: 'If you involve too many people, you get a multitude of voices. But if you don't involve enough then it can come back to haunt you – those left out may say "you didn't involve us" and create problems later.'

A TIP:

"Make sure you have an editorial board with the authority to push back and reject content."

FTSE 100 company secretary

Plan your photography

Depending on the type of company, or the design of your report, you may need little or no photography. But it's important to call it out as part of the planning process, because if you do need it then it has to be planned early – and ideally thought about throughout the year. 'It's essential that you don't leave it to the last minute – it's so annoying if you've had the perfect photo opportunity but you didn't take it!' says a REIT company secretary. 'And you should build up a good photo library.' Don't forget Board/exec photography – it's not essential but most companies include photos of their Board, and sometimes of executive team members. This needs careful planning, and usually takes place around a Board meeting. Make sure you choose an early Board meeting so that, if anyone's missing, there's an opportunity to photograph them later.

> When it comes to comments, make sure people understand the difference between a draft (in Word) and a proof (a designed PDF) so they know what they're going to be looking at. And be clear what you're asking for when seeking comments – what is in their remit to comment on and what isn't? This is particularly important when it comes to tone and style – be clear with people if you're just asking for factual accuracy, or they may try to rewrite things the way they would do it, and undermine the readability and consistency of your report. Also, don't forget to ask contributors to keep the principle of fair, balanced and understandable in mind – even if something's accurate it needs to be put into context; for example, a case study should not be given undue prominence if it's not merited.

4 And be ready to manage a changing process

With your preparation and planning done, you'll be in good shape to start the annual report project. But all that work could be wasted if you don't manage the process well – which, when it comes to annual reports, is about managing people, not tasks. As noted above, most of the people involved have other jobs, and the annual report is not their priority, so as project manager, you have to be able to get them to do what's needed and when.

No annual report schedule ever goes entirely to plan. Dates for drafts come and go; people are late with comments; senior people change their minds about things; results don't quite come in as planned. But ultimately the key deadlines still need to be met. In a time-sensitive environment your project manager must therefore be calm, communicative, diligent – and likeable, since he or she will need to persuade people to do things under pressure. But the ability to be forceful when necessary is also essential to ensure the work gets done and the report is progressing to plan. He or she needs to be into the detail but also able to step back and see the bigger picture. In Chapter 5, you'll find more on people and project management in the context of working with your agency; here are some key points for project managers dealing with their internal team.

Make sure lines of communication are open
Annual reports go through many iterations up and down the chain of command and to and from the auditors. And, however much preparation and planning has gone into the process, it's likely that there will be some setbacks. Good communication and resolution mechanisms are therefore essential for a smooth process.

- **Weekly meetings or calls** are useful for the working party, with more frequent meetings when you get near the end. Including the auditors in some of the meetings can be helpful to identify and avoid any roadblocks in getting the necessary information to them and making sure everything is on track. Ask a senior stakeholder to come along to meetings if there have been problems, so they can support you in getting things back on track.

- Make sure you have an **effective feedback loop** to capture general feedback and specific comments accurately, and to communicate back to contributors if their comments are overruled. There is nothing more annoying for a contributor than to have a later proof sent back without their comments included, and not to know whether that's because their comments were missed or because they were left out deliberately. In the words of one FTSE 100 company secretary: 'We had to let the content be a bit less good this year to mend the bridges with senior people who were unhappy with the way their feedback was handled last year.' So, make sure it's clear who is responsible for communicating back, how comments are to be collated, and how you are going to complete the loop with contributors.

Make technology work for you
Technology can ease the pain of marking up rounds of comments and keeping an up-to-date proof. It may not work for everyone, but software packages like CtrlPrint that enable you to edit directly in the designed document can significantly streamline the process. But be careful: you need to restrict access to such systems to a small group of people; otherwise, despite the ability of these systems to record every change, you may lose track of who has commented on what, and how their comments have been dealt with (see feedback loop above).

Link up with other year-end processes
It's important to remember that the annual report is not a standalone year-end process. It is inextricably linked to the preliminary or final results announcement and the investor presentation, and all three need to be joined up. Because there may be different owners for each document, the onus on communication becomes even more important. Make sure, then, that any annual report comments relevant to the other documents are fed back to the appropriate people, and make sure that the owner(s) of the annual report are plugged in to comments on the announcement and presentation. Many companies also copy and paste the results statement, or parts of it, into the annual report, so it's essential the content, tone and style are consistent – often a problem if they are not written by the same people.

There are also the ancillaries to think of – the notice of AGM, the proxy card, a letter to shareholders and indirect investors notifying them of the availability of those documents.

On a related point, ensure that there is sufficient verification of non-audited numbers and key statements – don't forget that the report, when taken as a whole, must be fair, balanced and understandable, and this applies as much to non-audited as to audited information.

And don't forget that the annual report content can – and should – form the foundation of how you communicate across all your channels. At the very least, it'll provide factual information that will be needed for updating your website. For more on making the most of your investment in the annual report and using content in other channels, see Chapter 6.

If in doubt, check (and check, check, and check again)
The annual report goes through multiple people and multiple iterations. By the time it's ready for publication, it's had so many pairs of eyes over it, including, no doubt, proof readers, that it's easy to think that nothing could possibly have slipped through. But, if you're in any doubt at all, about anything at all, it's always worth checking. If there is a niggle in your mind, it probably has some foundation – something you meant to look up and forgot. So give it another read. And make sure you check the spine for the print version – on the standard PDF you don't see the spine, so it's easy to miss. 'Last year no one had checked, and the spine had the same artwork from the previous year,' says a FTSE 100 company secretary. 'It was a really stupid mistake and we had to redo all the covers!'

5 Don't underestimate the approval process

Most companies will have various stages of approval for their annual report – the larger the company, the more complex, typically. For any company, the Board, Audit Committee and auditors will need to sign it off, but you may also have an internal body such as a disclosure committee or editorial committee. You may also have to manage a legal review, either by internal or external lawyers. Make sure you know the dependencies, and tee up the various bodies in your planning process, as noted above.

Get Audit Committee approval

In many companies, it's the Audit Committee, on behalf of the Board, that reviews the annual report and accounts to approve it as being fair, balanced and understandable. This Committee is responsible for recommending the financial statements to the Board for approval as well as reviewing certain sections of the front end. It is therefore well placed to consider whether the front end and back end are consistent. The Committee is also privy to the auditors' feedback on whether all material points have been included.

As well as the content of the report and financial statements, the Committee may also want to review your internal procedures for ensuring that the report complies with legal requirements – for example, the process you have followed throughout drafting and reviewing to make sure that all material information has been included and the report is fair, balanced and understandable.

> **IS IT FAIR, BALANCED AND UNDERSTANDABLE?**
>
> 'FBU' is a principle required by the UK Corporate Governance Code, and as such applies to premium listed companies, although it's a good principle for all companies to follow. From a practical point of view, then, you should ensure that you have a robust sign-off process that is sufficient to satisfy the Audit Committee and/or Board that the final report is indeed FBU. You need to be able to demonstrate that you've communicated the requirement to everyone drafting and reviewing the report, and that they've kept it in mind throughout the process. And, you need to ensure that all facts are checked – to prove something is fair, you need to be able to prove it is true.

But why is it that the regulators ask us to make reports FBU? Chapter 1 covers this in some detail, but in essence it's about reports being open and honest, while being accessible to stakeholders, thus engendering trust. However, too many annual reports you read today – including in the FTSE 100 – are verbose, boring and hide behind boilerplate language, which is entirely counter to the spirit of this regulation, even if they technically meet its letter or legal definition. This is why, from the perspective of the spirit of regulation, the guidance in Chapter 4 on writing and design is so important. So, when you're considering whether your report is FBU, look at it from the reader's perspective. And get people to help you. 'We get people who aren't involved in the report to read it at a late stage to check if it's fair, balanced, and understandable,' says a FTSE 100 company secretary from the utilities sector. 'They need to be people with an overview of the Group who will have a bit of knowledge about and interest in reporting, but who aren't part of the reporting team.'

Get Board approval

Once the Audit Committee has approved it, the annual report and accounts will then be put to the Board for approval at the same time as the results announcement, which is why it is so important to keep any changes after this to a minimum (i.e. correcting factual errors or typos that have been missed). Board packs tend to be circulated electronically nowadays, but since people tend to print off and read long documents (if they're going to read them thoroughly, that is) then giving them a hard copy will often get a better result.

Final sign-off

In practice, the Board may delegate final approval to a company disclosure committee or Board sub-committee to allow for minor changes to be made between the Board meeting and the date of the announcement. After the announcement, there is usually a small window of time to do a final proofread, check the printers' proofs and make sure everything is in order – although some companies do publish the report on the same day as the results, particularly dual-listed companies that have to meet non-UK legal requirements. Be aware, however, that once your auditor has signed the audit opinion, you will not be able to make any changes to the signed version of the report, other than fixing obvious typos or small grammatical errors – many auditors will not even allow you to change the order of words or bullet points. Also be aware that you need to allow at least two days, safer three, for your final proof read (for the average annual report), plus a day to implement, check and sign off any late corrections. Many people seem to think you can read an entire annual report in just a day, but, with reports running into hundreds of pages now, it's simply not possible.

Some notes on production

Chapter 6 has a discussion about how to use your annual report content in other ways, particularly online. For the purposes of this section, we're assuming that production means a) publishing a PDF on your website, b) creating the tagged ESEF version and c) print and distribution.

Publishing the PDF online

Publishing the PDF on your website is pretty straightforward – but make sure that the file is labelled properly. Too many annual report PDFs, when they're downloaded from companies' websites, have incomprehensible titles – 370_FINAL_ar2019 for example – which clearly reflect the internal production filing system, rather than what's going to be of use to the reader. The principle here is the same as everything else we've discussed – make it easy for your reader. And that means giving it a nice obvious file name like 'COMPANY_NAME_AnnualReport_DATE'.

Interactive PDFs – i.e. those with internal links that allow you to jump to different pages, for example by clicking on a title in the contents list – are standard today, although not all companies provide them. They are extremely useful, so do make sure you factor that in – they are not expensive to produce, and make life considerably easier for your reader.

And don't forget to update other parts of your website

If you don't have the co-ordinated communications approach based around the annual report story we advocate in Chapter 6, at the very least you'll need to update various parts of your corporate website to reflect any new information or facts about the company. So make sure you plan that into your production process.

Creating the tagged ESEF version

ESEF is the European Single Electronic Format, a new requirement for filing your full annual report as a tagged XHTML document (to enable its readability by machine readers) that came into force for reporting periods beginning on or after 1 January 2021. As you'll know if you've read the ESEF case study in Chapter 2, there was a lot of consternation around ESEF and what it would mean for the way annual reports are produced, not least concerns around the readability by human readers of XHTML documents if the ubiquitous, reader-friendly PDF format had to be abandoned.

Fortunately, our technical colleagues have found a way of converting the PDF format into XHTML, so the impact of ESEF on the annual report process has been minimised, although the practical implications for sign-off and audit processes are, at the time of writing, still being ironed out. Nonetheless, the process of tagging is a complicated exercise, and needs careful planning with the finance team, who are, of course, responsible for the financial statements, and whichever partner you choose to work with. As discussed in more detail on page 95, there are a number of approaches to producing the ESEF, with various external agencies offering different solutions. Like every other aspect of reporting, finding the right partner is about determining what skills and expertise you need to bring in to complement your in-house team, while ensuring that any partner has the right ethos and attitude to work well with you.

Print and distribution

Now that the days of print runs into the millions are a thing of the past, print is often considered to be a bit of an afterthought in the reporting process. After all, most people read it online, don't they? Don't fall into that trap – even if you're only printing a small number of copies. Inherent in the print process is the all-important final checking and sign-off (once printed, it's expensive to change), not to mention that the physical copies tend to hang around in corporate HQ and be referenced year after year.

If you don't have your own print manager to worry about these things for you, do keep the guidance on print production set out on pages 146-148 to hand throughout the process. After all, you don't want to open your box of beautiful copies and find last year's date printed on the spine...

Fail to prepare, prepare to fail...

ADDENDUM

How to tackle reporting when working remotely

by Claire Bodanis

As a result of the Covid-19 pandemic, we've all now experienced the challenges of remote working, and the additional burden this places on getting the annual report done at all, let alone done well. A freelance proof reader who works on many UK plc annual reports said that, during the 2020 season, he was having to make twice as many corrections as usual in some reports he was reading, and the general standard of copy was much lower.

There are all sorts of reasons why working on reports in the first half of 2020 was particularly difficult, which had nothing to do with reporting itself – the experience of total homeworking which was unfamiliar to many; heavier workloads because of furloughed colleagues and managing Covid-19 comms; plus the added challenges for many people of homeschooling children, social isolation and the level of personal stress and worry that it all brought with it. Nonetheless, while many of these challenges have now been overcome, remote working itself has made reporting much more difficult. Back to our freelance proof reader who told us that the issues he saw in 2020 were not just a one-off due to the immediate challenges of adapting to remote working in the middle of the annual report process. The 2021 season wasn't much better, which suggests that remote working itself adds complexity to the annual report process.

It seems likely, however, that office working as we know it is not going to return any time soon, and that various forms of remote working may become the norm for the next year or so, and possibly longer. There are particular challenges for reporting that will remain if some form of remote working becomes the new normal. If you work in a global company, you'll no doubt already be familiar with much of this, since involving people in different locations already requires virtual working – although of course it's rare that there isn't a core team sitting together in one location.

So what does remote working mean for the annual report project, and how we can make the experience work better for us and for reporting as a whole? This is particularly important because, with so much uncertainty in the world, high-quality, open and honest reporting will be more essential than ever.

This section is by no means a comprehensive study or guide to remote working. What we're aiming to do is share the main challenges we faced in reporting that arose from remote working, and give some practical suggestions for how to overcome them given that remote working in some form is set to continue. The first thing to say, though, is that the five key stages covered in this chapter, and the absolutely critical role of planning, are even more important when trying to manage a report at arm's length. And everything takes longer, which is why it's no surprise that our proof reader colleague found so many more errors in the 2020 and 2021 reports he was reading.

Let's look at the technical and practical challenges first. Many are IT-related, and the problems are compounded for those used to working in offices. Even after more than a year of remote working, many still lack the internet bandwidth and the hardware and software available in most corporate offices. More significantly, they also lack the immediate support of a member of the IT team who knows their system inside out.

Challenge 1: the technology for dealing with long documents

Many annual reports today run to hundreds of pages. Reading a document of that length on screen is not easy; try comparing lots of pages at once, and it becomes almost impossible. The most you can probably do at a size large enough to read easily is two or three pages; perhaps a few more if you're lucky enough to have lots of screens. Some people may live close enough to the office to have copies printed and couriered out, but many don't – and this will add time to an already shortened process, which is also why posting overnight may not be an option either. If you're properly set up for homeworking you may have printers and scanners good enough to print that number of pages, and to deal with the scanning too, but most people don't. The usual recourse for the homeworker of getting your local print shop to do it for you is also off the list for corporate reporting, given the sensitivity of the documents.

Many people don't have the right software to deal with adding comments and suggested edits to PDFs either. And most people who work for listed companies can't just go online, buy and install software – or even install free software – but instead have to negotiate the minefield of IT departments and purchasing, which often takes too long and gets so complicated that it becomes impossible. Some of our 2020 clients – and even some of our 2021 clients – had to resort to taking photos of marked-up pages on their mobiles and sending each page as a JPEG file, which takes both them and the agency ages to manage (see more on costs below).

What to do

It's all in the planning. Work out at the start who is going to need access to printers, scanners and proofing software, and get it set up before the start of the process. Depending on companies' budgets and locations, you may consider a combination of the following (noting that you may need time to get expensive printers through procurement):

- Get people set up with a high-quality printer and scanner for their home
- Make sure everyone has the necessary editing software on their work laptop
- Don't forget that marked-up scans become very large files, so people will need high-speed broadband and enough bandwidth to manage them (more on that in file storage below)
- Ensure you have someone in the office at the right times to print and courier copies when needed.

Challenge 2: version control and file storage

Many companies will have filesharing systems set up already, particularly in response to people working at home during the pandemic. Remote working makes these systems more important than ever, for a number of reasons. First, version control – when people aren't together in an office, they often don't know what each other is doing, and we've seen many instances where different people have been working on the same file, creating multiple versions, with resulting chaos and comments getting lost. This of course can happen when everyone's in the same office, but it seemed to become more of an issue while people were working remotely. It's really important to be rigorous about who's working on what and when – and perhaps to use a filesharing system so that everyone can always see what the latest version is. Second, security. Many companies do allow emailing of sensitive information and documents, but many don't, while some companies' firewalls block large file transfer systems like zip files or WeTransfer.

What to do
- Set up a cloud-based filesharing system, or a secure project folder within your company's existing system that's accessible only by the report project team.
A (secure!) filesharing system means you can send people a link when documents are ready to be shared, rather than emailing them – and it also circumvents the problem of enormous files clogging up email systems.
- Remember to make sure the system allows sharing by people outside the company, so that your agencies, auditors and so forth can access them.
- Create a protocol for file naming and working on the various documents, and make sure everyone's aware of it and follows it to avoid version control problems.
- If you want (and are allowed) to email files, make sure to password-protect sensitive ones, and always share the password in a separate email.
- Find out what the broadband speed and bandwidth is at people's homes, and upgrade if needed or invest in back-ups like dongles. This is particularly important when more than one person is working remotely from the same house, which can cause problems with connectivity.

Challenge 3: editorial (and proof) reading remotely

We've always thought that reading out loud[1] is best done together, in pairs, with your colleague in a room. So we were pleasantly surprised to discover in 2020 that it actually works quite well over a platform like Zoom, as long as you get yourself properly organised in advance, and people's home broadband can cope with it. Bear in mind that it can be more tiring to do out-loud reading online, so you may need to allow more time. There's also the added time and process of getting any handwritten comments to whoever is implementing them if it's a different team. But again, with good organisation and planning this can be done.

What to do
- Plan more time in your schedule for the various reads to allow for the extra time remote working requires.
- Agree in advance who's marking up amends, whether on paper or via PDF sticky notes, and how they're going to be passed to whoever is implementing them. In person you can just swap piles of paper, but of course you can't virtually, so it's more efficient if one person marks up, even if the reading itself is shared.
- Arrange delivery of hard copy proofs, or ensure people have the ability to print them off at home (see challenge 1, above).
- When reading over something like Zoom, consider switching off cameras and only turning them on to say hello and goodbye, and when you need to discuss things or are having a tea break. This makes it less tiring, minimises distractions and takes up less bandwidth.

The point about online rather than in-person meetings being more tiring is an important one, and has wider implications for the project as a whole, as discussed in the next couple of points, which are more about personal rather than practical challenges.

---

1 If you're not familiar with the concept of the out-loud, editorial read, this is when the writer (or writers) reads the report out loud in pairs with another member of the client team. It is by far the best and easiest way to check a report's readability as well as the accuracy of the language. It's usually done on the penultimate proof before Board sign-off, ie so that it's late enough to have incorporated the majority of comments and changes, but not too late to rewrite parts that don't read well.

Challenge 4: engaging and managing people you can't see

One of the most common complaints from people working remotely is that you can't just pop your head round someone's door and ask a question about, say footnote 3 on page 92. And because you can't see them, you don't know what they're doing, whether they're free to speak, what kind of mood they're in – so things that are usually quick and easy take more thought, more consideration of others, more planning, more time. It's harder to get people together in an ad hoc way, and the understanding of what's going on that happens by virtue of everyone being together just doesn't happen. This means you need to communicate much more – ideally with conversations rather than yet another email adding to an overflowing inbox – about what's going on in the project, so things don't get missed.

All this means more virtual meetings – but these tend to be harder work than those in person. You can't read the room in the same way as you can in person, so you need to concentrate far harder on what people are saying, while also looking out for any physical cues that it is possible to see. Similarly, you need to be much more careful yourself about how you come across so that others understand you. You also don't get the individual interactions between people that are so helpful in a meeting room, and take the pressure off the group. All this, plus having to look at yourself while you're looking at others, can make virtual meetings more tiring, while also taking longer to get the same things done. Some people do of course prefer virtual meetings, but the general consensus we heard over the last year or more of remote working was that not being able to meet in person was much harder and more tiring over the course of the project as a whole.

What to do

- Communicate more – schedule more catch-up calls or meetings, and include time at the start to catch up with how people are in themselves, since you can't see that for yourself, while respecting people's time. Not everyone wants to chat.
- Manage amends by scheduling group calls with everyone involved. 'Page turns' of the report with key content owners are standard practice, but you may want to

schedule extra ones to bring people together to discuss amends. This might seem like it would take longer, but in practice it saves time and avoids the frustration of seemingly endless emails as wording goes back and forth.
- Take the pressure off the visual – if you all know each other well, audio-only calls can be less tiring, so alternate with those, while remembering that if you can't see people you can't pick up the visual clues of how they are.
- Think about your setting for a video call: simple things like making sure you're sitting in good light, and are looking straight at the screen, rather than in front of a window with the top of your head cut off, for example, make the experience much easier for everyone else, who may find it distracting.

Challenge 5: attention from the right people at the right time

Another challenge a number of people mentioned about remote working was getting senior people's attention at the right time. In early 2020, this was no doubt a result of corporate leadership needing to deal with the immediate problems of Covid-19, but it's an issue that has continued. This goes to the heart of one of the key problems of poor reporting, which is the lack of senior leadership engagement. And it's something that only gets worse when more urgent things come onto the management agenda. Working remotely makes this more challenging, because it's far harder to get senior people's attention (particularly those who are uninterested in reporting) when you can't see them and therefore time your question by catching them on the way to the lift, or as they go between other meetings.

What to do

Unfortunately, there's no practical way to address this challenge. It just emphasises the importance of the points discussed in stages 1 and 2 of the main part of Chapter 3, about getting your leadership involved, and early. The more convinced they are of the importance of reporting, the higher up their agenda it will go. And the more they understand about the process, and the costs and other consequences of not engaging when needed, the more likely they are to give you their attention when you need it.

Challenge 6: keeping focused

Reporting requires concentrated effort and focus over long periods, particularly when it comes to drafting and proofing. And maintaining the laser-like focus needed to get the report over the line was the biggest challenge of all during the 2020 lockdown. Working from home in less constrained circumstances should ease the pressure somewhat, but it can still be difficult to focus for hours at a time without the support of the office environment and colleagues around you.

What to do

Everyone's home circumstances are different, and there's no one-size-fits-all solution here. Being aware of what helps you to focus and what distracts you should enable you to plan what's going to work best for you. For example, if the only time you can get sustained hours of concentration is late at night or early in the morning when other people are asleep, plan for it, and give yourself the time to sleep at the other end of the day. Or, as some people who work remotely all the time do, you could create your own 'office' with a colleague or two, by connecting over Zoom or Teams, and work with them virtually sitting next to you on mute, with a check-in every hour or so as agreed in advance. That way you get the feeling of being in an office with colleagues, even though you're not actually interacting – and seeing each other focusing on work can really help you do the same.

The final challenge covers the implications of all of these things for how you work with your agency (see Chapter 5 for more on working with your agency, including a discussion of budgets).

Challenge 7: added costs

Because remote working means longer hours for you, it will usually mean longer hours for your agency as well – and for agencies, time is money. More corrections because messaging keeps changing, and people find it harder to focus; more meetings to keep communication going; extra tasks given to your agency, such as text corrections or content management that would usually be done by someone in your team. As discussed in Chapter 5, you should always factor contingencies in the budget into each stage of the project, but, with remote working continuing, it's a good idea to increase this to avoid surprises at the end of the project.

And a potential challenge: developing ideas together, virtually

There are some stages of the report which, in our experience, have to be done in person to be effective – getting together round the table to come up with ideas for content and design, for example. Because of the timing of Covid-19, we haven't had the personal experience of having to do these remotely yet – and perhaps we won't have to. But if we do, then it's worth thinking about how to create an environment that's conducive to this kind of thinking, and the intense mental focus and energy that's required to get the best out of it. Some suggestions:

- **Find the right time of day and book the meeting for more time than you'll need.** People have to be able to focus so discuss with the team when would work best for them, and also allow extra time so that you can allow a period of time at the beginning for people to switch off from what they were doing before, and get into the right frame of mind.

- **Have a ceremonial start – and close off all other communications.** If people are keeping an eye on the phone, on emails, on other things, they simply won't have the clarity of mind to give the best input. Some kind of ceremonial start to the meeting when people switch off everything else except their meeting connection might help here.

- **Appoint someone to run the meeting and be comfortable with periods of silence.** These kind of sessions often don't have an official 'chair', but when you're working virtually you need one. Silence for thinking is essential in creative development and occurs naturally when you're in a room together, but can feel unnatural in a virtual meeting. A good chair will help this happen smoothly.
- **Be efficient with time, and if you finish early, stop!** People are always grateful to get time back in their day, so keep the session focused on the task in hand, and when you've got as far as you can, stop. Don't feel you need to use all the time set aside if people have run out of steam.

This may all seem rather daunting – and it's true that reporting, along with many other corporate projects, is much easier when you can work with people in person. But our experience so far has revealed some positives. Enforced homeworking, in our experience, prompted people to be more open and honest with each other, and to get onto a closer, more personal level more quickly. After all, although most people finally got themselves equipped with slick digital backgrounds, we've literally seen inside others' houses and, sometimes, 'met' their children. This kind of personal experience brings people together and helps with the single-team mentality that's so conducive to working well together.

What's more, 20 years ago when I started in reporting, it would have been practically impossible for all office workers to work at home, have no physical contact with people outside their household, and get an annual report out accurately and on time. Working lives for office workers too would have ground to a halt during lockdown, wreaking even more damage on society and the economy.

Technology means we can talk to each other face to face, individually and in groups, even if we're not in the room. It means we can do mark-ups and scans of proofs, even if it's more difficult and complicated. It means we can share files, even enormous ones. It means we can still do the essential out-loud read with each other, even if we can't share the chocolate biscuits. It means we can get the job done. And now that we know it's a scenario to contend with, we can plan it into our annual report process from the very beginning. ∎

Fail to prepare, prepare to fail...

A!

To recap

Checklists have their place, and this list of principles is a useful one to keep in mind during the reporting process. If you have to manage the project remotely as well, these principles become even more important.

- Define the purpose of your report
- Prepare absolutely everything
    - Get the right reporting agency (if using one)
    - Review last year's report
    - Benchmark it against your peers
    - Check for new requirements
    - Start with a blank sheet of paper
    - 'Cut the clutter'
    - Get your leadership on board
- Plan your project in minute detail
    - Set a detailed timetable
    - Create a team
    - Be clear about their responsibilities
    - Plan your photography
- Be ready to manage a changing process
    - Make sure lines of communication are open
    - Make technology work for you
    - Link up with other year-end processes
    - If in doubt, check (and check, check and check again)
- Don't underestimate the approvals process
    - Get Audit Committee approval
    - Get Board approval
    - Final sign-off
- Don't let production be an afterthought, especially not print! Changes can get expensive...

The three stages of print production

With thanks to print manager Liz Grahame of The Printed Page Limited for sharing her secrets with us.

STAGE 1 – PLANNING AND PAPER CHOICE

- Produce the production timetable (in discussion with your printer, your agency and your registrar) but make sure you factor in some contingency time for both you and your printer before the posting date.
- Compile a print specification and send it to your printer
- Ask your printer to produce paper dummies of different paper options (i.e. bound books of blank paper made up to the approximate length of your annual report) so you can tell what the final document will look/feel like.
- Discuss the environmental credentials of the paper, printing and finishing options – very important when your report probably has a discussion of the company's environmental impacts.
- Review print costs from your chosen printer for all items and benchmark prices against other printers.
- Review the mailing matrix and compile specifications for all the ancillary items (notice of meeting, proxy card etc) – not forgetting the polywrap and/or envelopes, and again considering the environmental impact of the outer packaging.
- Review postage costs and class.
- Check the weight of the report plus ancillary items to ensure it is within the most cost-effective postage bands.
- Choose and order your paper – ensure that you have allowed enough sheets (of paper), since a reprint is very costly; aside from the shareholder mailing remember to factor in file copies for you, any global offices you may have, your agency/other partners, and any other distribution lists.

Fail to prepare, prepare to fail...

STAGE 2 – TESTING ARTWORK

- Your agency or your designer should prepare what's known as 'scatter proof' artwork – this is where images, graphics and other styles are 'scattered' on a sheet and then printed by your printer using the inks and paper you've chosen, on the printing machine that the report will be printed on. This is to test that graphics, colours and line weights print correctly and will be readable and clear – things can look very different when printed from what you see on screen. Following this, some photos may need to be retouched, for example to sharpen the image or improve people's skin tone, or colours on graphics may need to be tweaked.

- Your agency or designer should prepare 'book proof' artwork – this is where a medium/late (but not final) proof of the whole report is printed by your reporting printer and bound into a book on the correct paper, so you can see what the report will look like in its final form (usually digitally printed, however, to keep costs down). This gives you the opportunity to check the layout, spine and pagination, and also to check the weight of the paper. A common problem which the book proof will reveal is if copy or imagery is too close to the inner part of the page and 'gets lost in the gutter' (where the paper meets and is bound into the spine); doing the book proof gives you the opportunity to fix it in advance. Note: don't leave this too late – you need to have time to change the artwork if it doesn't look right.

- Your agency, designer or registrar should prepare test artwork for all the ancillaries, so any personalised items can be tested to make sure that the address is in the right position and all the correct size envelopes or polywraps have been ordered.

STAGE 3 – CHECKING FINAL PROOFS

- When your printer receives final artwork, they will produce a set of high resolution proofs for you to check. If you are printing litho rather than digitally (which comes down to cost and the length of the print run; digital print tends to be cheaper for shorter print runs), this will be done before the printers make the printing plates from which they will print the final document. It's important to check these carefully since any changes will be expensive. If your report is printed digitally, you don't need to worry about changes to printing plates, but even so, you still need to sign off the proofs. A good way to do this is by using 'traces', whereby your printer runs out your approved PDF file onto tracing paper as well; you can then lay this over each page of the high resolution proof and check that nothing underneath has moved or changed.
- Arrange to 'pass on press' – this is where you go to the printer on the first day of printing and check and sign off each sheet at the beginning of its print run.
- If you don't have a print manager, your printer should help you check that each sheet matches the scatter proof artwork you signed off in stage 2. If you have an agency, they should send their print manager or designer to check the proofs as well.

DON'T FORGET...

- Book your report in early with a printer since they get very busy during reporting season (although it's worth doing this even if you have an unusual year end).
- Book a logistics meeting at the start of the process with all suppliers as this will give you an opportunity to discuss all the items in stage 1 – this could save you money.
- Ensure that the paper you choose is easily available just in case you need more once the paper order date has passed, for example because of an increase in pagination or because extra copies are needed.
- Make sure you look at scatter proofs in proper daylight, because images may look very different depending on the lighting.
- Ensure that you get advance copies of all the other ancillary items that are going into the pack; some ancillary proofs are signed off from PDFs and don't always get checked properly.

Spotlight on dual-listed companies

Interview with Ben Mathews, Company Secretary, BP

Ben Mathews, Company Secretary of BP (listed on the UK and US exchanges with a legacy listing in Germany), talked to us about the benefits and challenges of managing reporting for a large dual-listed company.

Q – How do reporting requirements differ between the UK and US?

A – The entire system and approach to governance and reporting is very different. The US has a rules-based system while the UK's is principles-based. If you look at a US 20F (the annual report for foreign companies with a secondary listing in the US), you'll see it's basically a big form that you have to fill in, answering every question. The US system is about compliance with the black and white rules of disclosure obligations, which means it becomes more about what you shouldn't say rather than what you should say.

Personally, I have a lot of time for the UK's principles-based system, and I really like the 'comply or explain' approach to provisions in the Corporate Governance Code. Over the last 25 years, this has become a globally respected framework for reporting, because it allows you to report transparently what you need to as a company. Under this system, as long as the principle of fair, balanced and understandable reporting is respected, then for listed issuers there is some flexibility to make your reporting meaningful.

Q – Do you produce separate reports for different jurisdictions?
A – Not exactly, but we do produce a 20F 'wraparound' with our annual report, rather than a separate report as such.

Q – How do you make sure you produce a good UK annual report when dealing with multiple listing requirements?
A – In the UK, good reporting is about telling a story, essentially a qualitative exercise, while meeting disclosure requirements. The main problem is doing this while being mindful of litigation exposure in the US. While there are safe harbour provisions, the US lawyers are unsurprisingly much more cautious about what you say and are keen to reduce the qualitative element, so there is an inevitable tension.

Getting round this is about bringing people together to understand why the other needs to report in a certain way, and what the boundary lines are. By understanding each other's position it's easier to come together and compromise. Good planning is essential – you need to do this early so you can agree an overall framework within which to report.

Q – What advice would you give to a colleague managing dual-listed reporting?
A – Keep a constant eye on reporting regulation across all your jurisdictions. And it's not just the annual report – it's all the other regulatory announcements as well. For example, if you have new non-execs, the information you have to disclose about them and their biographies may be different in different jurisdictions.

> ❝ *By understanding each other's position (UK/US) it's easier to come together and compromise.* ❞

There are also different requirements about the timing of announcements. Hong Kong, for example, has timing windows within which you need to announce, while in the UK you can just publish when something is ready. Also bear in mind time zones – usually announcements need to be made at the same time in different places, which may mean being up at weird hours of the night to meet legal requirements elsewhere.

Q – Would you recommend dual listing?
A – That's a hard one! It's expensive, it's complex, it's challenging. And the statistics speak for themselves – there's an ever-decreasing number of companies coming to IPO at all, not just dual listings, because of the complexity and challenges associated with being a listed issuer, not least the exposure it brings. There's no shortage of money out there for investment, but many companies are looking for alternative means of raising capital – private equity for example.

In the old days everyone listed everywhere because it was great for a company's profile. But investors are beginning to question the value of a multi-listing because of the increasing regulatory cost. There's no doubt it's good for transparency, but it is an administrative and operational burden. If you want exposure in the US and China, though, then really you need to be listed there.

In the end, it will depend on your company's own circumstances, weighing up your need for capital from those markets against those costs. And that will be different for everyone. ∎

WHAT IS A DUAL-LISTED COMPANY?

A dual- or multi-listed company, sometimes also called a cross-listed company, is one whose shares are traded on two or more different exchanges. Well-known examples are BHP, BP, Diageo, Rio Tinto and Unilever.

WHAT ARE THE BENEFITS OF LISTING ON MORE THAN ONE EXCHANGE?

Typically, companies list on more than one exchange to get access to a larger pool of potential investors than is available in their domestic market. Listing in the US has historically been attractive to many non-US companies because of the depth of American capital markets. Dual listing can also improve a company's share liquidity and its public profile because the shares trade on more than one market. There may also be some instances where companies that want to operate in a new area have to list on a local exchange to demonstrate their commitment to that area.

AND THE DRAWBACKS?

Dual listing comes with significant challenges and costs, not least the requirement to comply with the sometimes very different corporate reporting requirements of different jurisdictions. And, different regulatory and accounting standards may mean companies need to hire extra legal and finance staff, as well as making more demands on management time, for example investor roadshows in more than one jurisdiction.

HOW HAS GLOBALISATION AFFECTED DUAL LISTING?

The benefits of dual listing seem to have fallen in recent years, as capital markets have globalised, becoming more liquid and integrated, and investors more global in their outlook. Also, the development of global online communications has given companies easier and cheaper ways of raising their profiles.

Spotlight on large private companies

Interview with Martin Ansley-Young, Company Secretary of Arup

Martin Ansley-Young is Company Secretary of Arup, a global firm of designers, engineers, architects, planners, consultants and technical specialists headquartered in the UK. Martin shared his views on reporting and its developing landscape for a large private company.

Q – Annual reports – pain or gain?
A – Up until a year ago, I'd have said that the annual report fell largely into the pain category – even though it gives us the comfort of an audited statement of record – mainly because of the lack of usefulness of much of what we have to include. Our statutory group accounts have grown from 30 pages to over 50, with much of the increase being gobbledegook around pension accounting and actuarial assumptions that adds nothing to a normal reader of accounts. This information may of course be valuable for pension actuaries, but it's just confusing for everyone else who isn't interested in it – so why put it in the annual report?

Q – So why is reporting becoming a bit more 'gain'?
A – The new governance reporting requirements are quite interesting because they're really making us reflect on how we work, why we do things in certain ways, and whether it would be good to do certain things

differently. For example, we're now putting a more formal structure around directors' training and some aspects of risk management. They've also made us realise that we should be telling our story better about the good things we do that are different – for example, we don't have personal incentive pay, and our leadership are on fundamentally the same remuneration structure as everyone else. Our profit sharing is global, based on the success of the group overall, which we think is hugely beneficial for getting people to act for the benefit of everyone, and not for short-term individual gain. This isn't the norm for many companies of our scale.

Q – Who reads your report – are there any crossovers with listed companies?
A – I need to qualify 'report' here. We have our statutory accounts, which are 'boring but useful' – when we're bidding for work, especially in the public sector, we need something independently verified to attest to our financial position. This is mostly how our statutory reporting is used. But we also publish a separate, non-statutory document which we call our annual report. This is where we tell our story, and include all the really important non-financial stuff that people want to know. It gets much closer to the heart of who we are, the expertise we bring, the projects we do. We give it to major clients and anyone else who wants to know about us – for example, architects, clients or collaborators who've not worked with us before – as well as people thinking of joining us, and we provide copies in all our office reception areas for casual readers. It's probably similar to the 'other stakeholders' audiences of listed companies; it's certainly not produced for the benefit of analysts or investors – because we don't have them!

❝ *The new requirements have made us realise that we should be telling our story better about the good things we do that are different.* ❞

Q – How will the new regulations affect your reporting?
A – It'll change the statutory accounts, since we will have to publish our response to the Code in that document. However, because we think it will say some interesting things about us we'll want to include it in our story report as well, which is going to take us back round the track of questioning whether it makes sense to produce two documents if there's a lot of overlap. But – we still want our annual report to be a really engaging story and we don't want the statutory stuff to distract from that! It seems to me that, in a digital world, the boundaries should be more fluid. We should be able to have lots of different material that we can assemble on the fly for different purposes so that we can use the right form of communication for different people. It is about time reporting caught up. ■

WHAT IS A LARGE PRIVATE COMPANY?

A private company is one whose shares may not be offered for sale to the public and are not traded on public exchanges. Typically, they are companies owned by their founders, or their management, or a group of private investors. Family firms are a good example. In terms of size, there is no one single definition of 'large' – it depends on the context. The Government uses different criteria depending on the context, but as regards new reporting requirements, there are three broad definitions:

- **Definition 1:** a company that has either or both of the following: more than 2,000 employees; and a turnover of more than £200 million with a balance sheet of more than £2 billion

- **Definition 2:** a company that has two or more of the following: turnover of more than £36 million; a balance sheet total of more than £18 million; and more than 250 employees

- **Definition 3:** a company with more than 250 employees in the UK.

All definition 1 companies will therefore also meet definition 2, although not necessarily definition 3.

HOW DO THEIR REPORTING REQUIREMENTS DIFFER FROM THOSE OF PUBLICLY LISTED COMPANIES, AND WHY?

In general, the reporting requirements for large private companies are less onerous than they are for public companies (i.e. they have to disclose less information). This is because private companies stem from private ownership, meaning that the providers of capital are looking after the money themselves as managers of the business – or at least, are close to the Board and management. Therefore these owners do not need a regime to protect their interests in the way that shareholders in public companies do, given that they are not directly involved in or close to the running of the company.

WHAT CHANGES TO THE REPORTING FRAMEWORK FOR LARGE PRIVATE COMPANIES ARE ON THE HORIZON?

This is beginning to change, however, and large private companies in the UK now have to report in far more detail, particularly around governance. There are four principal changes:

- **New Corporate Governance Statement**
  New Government legislation the Companies (Miscellaneous Reporting) Regulations 2018 requires all companies of a significant size (Definition 1 above) that are not currently required to provide a corporate governance statement to disclose their governance arrangements.

- **The Wates Corporate Governance Principles for Large Private Companies**
  In January 2018, the Government appointed James Wates CBE to chair an industry Coalition Group tasked with developing corporate governance principles for large private companies. James Wates is Chairman of his family firm, the Wates Group, one of the leading privately owned construction and property companies in the UK. The Coalition Group came up with six principles – purpose and leadership; Board composition; directors' responsibilities; opportunity and risk; remuneration; and stakeholder relationships and engagement – the aim of which is to provide 'a framework for ensuring that their companies are well managed and aligned behind a clear purpose'. These are not legal requirements, but useful guidance for a large company.

- **New section 172 statement requirement on directors' duties**
  Large private companies that meet Definition 2 (Definition 1 companies therefore also included) are currently required to publish a strategic report. They, like public companies, now also have to include in their strategic report a section 172 statement that explains how directors have met their duties under section 172 to promote the success of the company for the benefit of its members as a whole.

- **Disclosure of extent of engagement with suppliers, customers and relevant others**
  Requirements for the directors' report have been amended to include an explanation of how directors have engaged with employees, how they pay attention to employees' interests, and what impact that has had on their decision-making. They will also have to explain how they have engaged with suppliers, customers and others who have a business relationship with the company. This regulation will apply to all companies meeting Definition 3.

WHY THE CHANGES, GIVEN THE LACK OF PUBLIC INVESTORS?

The new legislation speaks to one of the themes we're seeing in reporting, which is that business is having to become accountable to a wider range of stakeholders beyond its investors (see a discussion of the changing purpose of business in Chapter 2). For large private companies, the issue is really to do with their size – there are some very large private companies today whose economic and social significance for wider stakeholders is just as large as that of a similar-sized public company. And greater, of course, than a much smaller public company.

It is worth noting that this move towards more disclosure for large private firms may continue to grow. In recent years the debate about the drop in IPOs and the flight of capital to private equity and its consequences for society as a whole has been gathering momentum, particularly in relation to how we will deal with the twin challenges of the fallout from Covid-19 and the ever deepening climate crisis. Over time, if the economic significance of large private companies grows, this may increase pressure for more prescriptive or enhanced reporting requirements to make sure that wider stakeholders' interests are protected.

CHAPTER 4

Respect your reader

How to make your report useful and engaging through writing and design

by Heather Atchison

Q?

Questions this chapter will answer

- Do corporate reports really need to be useful and engaging?
- What are the main causes of robotic, dull reporting – and how can they be overcome?
- What are the essential language techniques behind accessible reporting?
- How does good design make a difference?
- And how can you get the report in front of your readers?

A COMPLEX AND FREQUENTLY VARYING RANGE OF FACTORS exist pertinent to this particular subject, which serve to ensure that, in the context of corporate report writing, the desired readership often fails to adequately engage with or comprehend the fundamental narrative of this requisite enterprise publication.

Admit it, you were already thinking about flipping to the next chapter, weren't you? And yet, many annual reports are full of pages and pages of sentences of this ilk. But no one wants to wade through that kind of thing, and most people simply won't – even in a report. This chapter explains how to avoid creating this type of experience – and why making your report a useful and engaging read really does matter. And when we say report, we're talking about all of it – not just the strategic report. The governance report and financials have readers too, even if they tend to be more interested in looking up information; we need to make the experience engaging for them as well.

The bottom line
Annual reports exist for good reason. The many regulatory requirements governing reporting are there to make sure companies communicate clearly with stakeholders, particularly their shareholders, giving people a clear sense of what they do and how successful they are at doing it. And the best reports, in doing just this, engender trust and pride in the business.

You may, of course, see your report as purely a compliance exercise – as something no one really reads anyway. If so, do feel free to flick to page 183. But please don't be hasty, because this attitude usually leads to reports that are against both the spirit and the letter of the law. It's also, alongside the complexity involved in creating an annual report, one of the reasons reports are often held up as some of the worst examples of corporate communications: boring, uninspiring, confusing and badly written.

The UK's Financial Reporting Council (soon, we hope, to become the Audit, Reporting and Governance Authority, or ARGA) would have it otherwise. In recent years, they've advised that reports should:

- Tell a story – have something to say
- Be fair, balanced and understandable[1] – tell it in a way that can be understood
- Cut the clutter – be clear and concise, and include only material information
- Be innovative – have a voice.

If you really want to be compliant, your report does need to engage – and above all, to tell your story clearly. Chapter 1 explains what a story is in the context of an annual report and how to think about creating it; this chapter is about how to write and design that story, plus all the information the report needs to include, in a way that's useful and engaging.

Within the context of the story, the annual report needs a logical structure, with the right information clearly signposted and in the right places. Trust, after all, grows from clarity and consistency. You can do your level best to tick the regulatory boxes, but if people don't read or understand your report, you haven't fulfilled your obligations to communicate certain critical things about your business. And, ultimately, a report that makes your company seem inaccessible or evasive will reduce trust, not create it. This is why, in the words of a FTSE 100 company secretary, and echoed by many others, 'You should start with what you want to say, your own story, and then once you've done that, go back and do the box ticking to make sure you've covered everything. DON'T start with the regulations!'

---

1 Contributors often forget that this is actually a requirement of the UK Corporate Governance Code (which applies to premium listed companies), and is also included in the FRC's Guidance on the Strategic Report. So it makes sense to pay attention to it.

There are two levels to making a report useful and engaging. The first is to make it accessible – opening its content up to its (sometimes broad) readership. If reports are indeed the 'source of truth' about a business, that truth has to be findable and understandable, both at storytelling level and fact-finding level. And the second is to use language and design to make the report engaging and navigable, so that people a) want to read more, and b) can find what they're looking for. This chapter looks at how to do both.

Common culprits

But first, let's look at some of the things that stand in the way of useful, engaging reporting; some of the reasons reports so often feel corporate and robotic – ending up inspiring no one and informing only the few.

Writing and editing by committee

To some extent, writing by committee is unavoidable. Reports must be checked by auditors and signed off by the Board, and they need information from different parts of the company. But when a report is written by people with varying writing styles and abilities, and with no sense of the big picture – the key story, messaging and voice holding everything together – the outcome will be an inconsistent and often challenging read.

This is compounded by the fact that, in many cases, contributors to the report are busy people who know their subject, but not how to communicate it to someone who doesn't. As one company secretary puts it, 'They're often not particularly skilled at telling the organisation's story in a way that engages the reader, as they're too close to it and their skills lie in other areas, not annual report writing!'

Neglecting the basics of design

At its simplest, good design is the art of helping your reader through the report – amplifying and enhancing its messages, and making information easy to find for those who are using the report as a document of record, and are looking things up. Compromising the basics of design – for example, by putting too many words on each page or using a tiny text size for body copy – will create a report that feels impenetrable and/or overwhelming. It may be tempting to sacrifice word count limits down the line to speed up the process towards sign-off, but your readers will suffer if you do.

Extreme caution
Yes, reports are highly regulated documents. They do need checking by auditors and lawyers. And, to be balanced, they sometimes need to include information that contributors don't feel entirely comfortable about sharing externally. But none of this means they have to share paragraph after paragraph of immaterial detail, just to cover all the bases. Or couch messages in formal, wordy, often impenetrable language (see the first sentence of this chapter!).

But there can be a temptation to default to formal, corporate legalese, particularly when disclosing anything less than positive. In the words of one Fortune 500 reporting director: 'This is something lawyers get nervous about. The writers may try, but it's not uncommon to find a report falling back into impersonal language when talking about controversial issues. You know when the lawyer has provided the script.'

Going through the motions
A closely connected pitfall is writing to say (simply to meet the regulations) instead of writing to be understood, with the excuse that no one really reads the report. People do. Perhaps not word for word and cover to cover, but in various guises and in various places, as our various points of view throughout this book attest. As Andy Griffiths of The Investor Forum points out on page 213, people do read the annual report if 'a company has a problem and they want to find what was said about it', and 'the annual report is your one chance to tell a compelling, integrated story, and if you can do that, you'll draw shareholders to you'.

Project (mis)management
At the root of many of the reporting challenges (and failures) we see is a disregard for two critical things: process and people. Without clear roles and responsibilities, or a solid briefing to inform contributors about the year's narrative, voice and key messages, or a clear process with time built in for editorial review, or an effort to bring together design and content from the start, your report is unlikely to reflect well on your company. 'In the last few years we have put in place a couple of things that have made a big difference – mainly being a proper team,' comments a FTSE 100 company secretary, energy sector. 'This has led to a better dialogue about strategy and key themes; having

conversations with the right people; and, crucially, working closely together to make sure the report is consistent and the flow works.'

I know, of course, that I'm not telling you anything you're not already painfully aware of. The real question is how to overcome the barriers to writing clear and engaging reports. So here are some pointers for how to do just that.

Laying the ground for good reporting

This part of the chapter is not about the process or management of reporting (for that, see Chapter 3), or about how to work with a reporting agency (see Chapter 5), both of which can help to address the common culprits highlighted above. But here are a few critical things you can do to make sure your report tells the clear, compelling and consistent story explained in Chapter 1.

Use a good brief

A thorough brief lays out the direction for the content, messaging and structure of the annual report – and is the key to both process and people. It's a mechanism for thinking through what the report is aiming to communicate about the company and the year, and for reminding everyone of the kind of language people can expect to see. Shaping the brief is also a chance for everyone to sit round the table – building a sense of team and a shared understanding. It's a way of aligning the many people, often with varying perspectives, involved in reporting – both so that contributors are more likely to provide the right content in the first place, and so that drafts produced by the writer and/or editor are reviewed with an understanding of the agreed narrative and reporting voice.

Without this kind of understanding, people are much more likely just to repeat the kind of writing they use for themselves and their colleagues. So, a solid and well-communicated brief is one of the best ways to avoid the reporting ping-pong that sometimes happens between contributors and writers/editors – one team changing the language only to have it changed back again, and so on and so on.

A good brief also allows the designers to work on the visual presentation with an understanding of the story that needs to be told and the impressions that the report needs to create.

Here's how one FTSE 100 company secretary approaches the brief: 'It doesn't matter if you have different authors – as long as they can all write! But people need to know the big picture – the key story/message and what you want to get across – so that what they're writing hangs together. We get all key authors and designers in a room to discuss and agree the key themes, stories, investor story, overall structure, etc. Everyone has the same outline before they start.'

There are certain essential ingredients to a good brief, which you will find on pages 169-172. But whatever its contents, for a brief to have the desired effect it needs to have the right people involved in its creation, including your designers; be signed off by key reviewers (and anyone likely to derail the direction – so you need to get directors' input before it's signed off!); be used to steer contributors, designers and writers; and be used as a yardstick for measuring success.

A TIP:
Make sure your Board has approved the messages and the language style set out in your brief – otherwise you may have to deal with directors disagreeing, and trying to rewrite things in their own style. Many Boards of course delegate the report to a steering group of senior representatives (whether or not they really should), but even so, it's worth making sure of the Board if you can.

Aim for a single editorial voice
A single editorial voice doesn't necessarily mean your report needs a single writer. But it does need to have a consistent voice and style[1] – something that a good writer or editor can provide if involved in the right way and at the right time. Involving a writer from the start can, in fact, transform your report, whether that's a professional you bring in, or someone you identify within your team who can write well. They'll bring a clarity of thinking to the task that will show itself in the clarity of writing in your report. A good writer will act as a linguistic auditor –

Continues on page 172.

---

1 The exception to this is anything that's supposed to be directly in the voice of an individual. To feel authentic and believable, sections like the CEO or Chairman's statements should sounds like they come from those individuals.

The essential elements of a reporting brief

Audience

- Who's your main audience? The investors, may seem the obvious answer, but it's worth thinking more closely about who the investors are – and there may be many. Again, from Andy Griffiths: 'No two are the same, and no two will agree. On the institutional side, in an investment organisation, you have analysts, generalists, governance people... no one is likely to read all of a report.' And, of course, you may have retail shareholders, as well as the other audiences...

- Don't forget that reports today are read by a far wider group of stakeholders – employees, potential employees, NGOs, customers, and so on (see some surprising statistics in Chapter 1, page 36) – and you want it to be accessible to these groups, too.

A TIP:

When writing your report, focus on the people who are most likely to read it, while remembering to go back after you've written your story to check it meets your legal obligations too.

Objectives

- Beyond regulatory requirements, what, in particular, are you trying to achieve with this year's report in terms of communication objectives? You may want to structure this by audience.

- You may also have project objectives for the reporting team, such as reducing the burden of reporting on the organisation.

Key messages

There are generally two types of messages for an annual report – the ongoing messages about the company, and the specific messages for the year. Remember, though, that the messages defined in the brief aren't those that should be repeated verbatim in the report – they're things you want the reader to think about your business, having read it. So:

About the business

- What are the main impressions or feelings you want to create in the reader?
- What do you want people to understand about your business from reading the report?

About the year

- What are the specific messages about the year that need to be included?

A TIP:

Remember to include that the report must be 'fair, balanced and understandable'. Reminding contributors that this is a legal requirement will encourage them to resist their natural urge just to talk about the good stuff.

Copy/editorial approach

- What tone of voice do you want to use in the report? A few examples of what this looks like (and doesn't look like) can be very useful.
- How is this similar to/different from your company's general brand voice? The annual report should be consistent with your brand voice even if there are some differences in emphasis.
- Are there specific voice or style guidelines that your writers should follow? These may be part of your brand guidelines.

A TIP:

If you don't have tone of voice guidelines, you should at least establish some principles for the annual report to guide your writer – particularly important if there are multiple writers.

Content plan

Think through the logic of your story, page by page – and list this in the brief (or in a separate document if this gets too unwieldy). Include the purpose/aims of each section. As a former auditor, now reporting consultant, advises (and this was echoed by many company secretaries we spoke to), 'it's best to start by telling your story the way you want to tell it, then go back and check you've covered everything. It also makes a better read'.

A TIP:

Don't let the statutory information you have to provide interrupt the narrative flow of your report. In the governance report in particular, gathering all the tick-box stuff in one place is a useful way of making sure it doesn't derail your reader.

Design, channels and format

- **Channel:** how will people access and read the report? Aside from the regulatory print and ESEF requirements, and the standard PDF download on your website, will you be creating any kind of microsite or summary? Remember that many people will download your annual report and look at it on screen, or print off sections, so be cautious about using things that work well in print but less so online, such as fold-out covers, or lavish use of double-page spreads. And, how will you make sure that the messaging across the rest of your website is in line with what's in the annual report?

- **Visual assets:** what scope does the design team have for developing new visual assets for the annual report? Bear in mind that, to tell the annual report story well, what you have in your existing library may not be enough. Nonetheless, do provide any brand guidelines and access to internal photo libraries/infographics etc.

- **Photography:** if you're going to do a photo shoot for the report, make sure you work with your agency and photographer to create the right brief specifically for the shoot.

- **Word counts/page counts:** what are the word and page count limits? These may not have been established yet – they tend to come with the design concept. But if you have any requirements at this stage, they should be included in the brief. Try not to be straitjacketed by previous years here – don't forget that lighter content spread over more pages can transform a report and make it feel shorter and more readable, even if there are more pages, while, of course, being mindful of paper and print costs, particularly if you have a large print run.

- **Format:** what is the page size for printed reports/ downloadable PDFs (A4, American Quarto, etc)? Do you have a requirement for the type of paper, for example the percentage of recycled content, or whether the cover laminate will be recyclable? Getting the advice of a print manager, either directly or through your reporting agency, can be hugely valuable, and may save you money as well (see Chapter 3, pages 146-148 for more on print).

A TIP:
Now that most people access annual reports as PDFs online, when thinking about format, it's important to consider that experience. Think about how easy or otherwise it is to read it on screen, and also what it will look like if people print it off themselves.

Logistics/process milestones
Your brief should also cover high-level process, sign-off and logistics – discussed in Chapter 3.

In summary... what does success look like?
It's useful to ask yourself what would make you think, when the report is published 'ah, that was a great project, I'm really proud of our annual report'. If you can define that, it will help guide everyone working on it.

pulling people up when they're hiding behind jargon. They'll become your company's conscience – pushing you to tell your story through language that's open and accessible. They'll ask hard questions: Why is this here? What does this mean? Is this fair, balanced and understandable?

There's an added benefit too, as Andrew Ninian of The Investment Association says (see pages 217-219): 'Having to write things down... helps you develop your thinking around an issue, and therefore how you are going to manage it.'

So, finding a talented writer/editor (whether in-house or not) who will challenge your thinking and put a deft hand to the language of your report is one of the keys to effective reporting.

If your company already has a brand voice, documenting how this will apply to the reporting context – and giving contributors examples of what this looks like – can help you get better quality content from the business. Taking the time to define the voice you want to use when reporting (and creating a style guide covering all relevant elements) will smooth the way to consistency. And don't forget to join up with the results statement writer, if that person is different from the person writing the annual report. Many companies flow their results statement into their annual report, which can have pretty disastrous consequences for the reader's experience if they are inconsistent in content, message or tone (and they often are).

Be brave – rein in the legalese
We've seen many a beautifully written report's carefully crafted words skewered at the eleventh hour by a Board director or lawyer. Remember, your lawyers are your advisors, not your masters. While you do of course need to be careful not to say something that could be misleading or used against you if you're in the middle of litigation, as long as what you're saying isn't legally wrong, and you haven't made a mistake, then it should be said in a way that's true to the voice of your report. In most cases, much of what lawyers advise companies not to say are the very things that everyone wants to hear – the unvarnished, unspun truth. Readers aren't stupid. They can tell when you're trying to hide something. Good lawyers know that – as you can read in 'a lawyer's view' on pages 59-63.

Get your language basics right

Your brand or reporting voice aside, there are four powerhouse language techniques that will give your report clarity and readability:

1. Keep sentences short and focused
2. Use everyday language, instead of internal or industry jargon
3. Be concise and to the point
4. Focus on people, using active verbs.

Even if you do nothing else, applying these will go a long way towards making your report useful and accessible to your many readers.

1 Keep sentences short and focused

This is one of the most common language problems we see in reporting: sentences which just don't know when to quit. Focusing sentences on one main point and keeping them to around 20 words doesn't just make them easier to follow, it will give your writing pace and energy. Squashing everything into one sentence to make the overall wordcount shorter doesn't necessarily aid readability or make the text feel shorter to the reader – in fact it can achieve the opposite.

> **So instead of a sentence like this one:**
>
> For both internal and external recruitment, we aim to position base salary at an appropriate level, taking into consideration a range of factors including the executive's current remuneration and experience, internal relativities, an assessment against the relevant comparator groups and cost.
>
> *(A 41-word sentence with a fair few points.)*

Write something like this:

Whether we're recruiting executives from within the company or beyond it, we aim to set base salaries appropriately. This means taking a range of factors into consideration. We look at the potential recruit's current salary, their experience, the salaries of our existing executives, an assessment of relevant comparator groups and cost.

(A 51-word paragraph, but with three sentences, far more readable.)

2 Use everyday language, instead of internal or industry jargon

If the aim of reporting is to be open and transparent about your business, aiming your storytelling at someone with little knowledge of your company or industry is a good way of making it accessible to all. This means using language that everyone can understand, which is why the FRC specifies that reports 'should be written in plain language'.

In the words of a FTSE 250 comms director: 'The biggest challenge when writing an annual report is to find a way to explain what a company does, and how successful it is at doing it, in a clear and simple way that can be understood by someone who has never come across the company before. It sounds easy enough but it's difficult to do, and the temptation to resort to 'corporate speak' or generic terms is strong. But the best annual reports find a way to make the complex simple to understand.'

This is not about 'dumbing down' your report; it's about opening it up. And clarity aside, using more everyday language in your report will help you come across as more human and believable.

This means moving from language like this: To this:

for the reason that	because
per annum	each year
terminate	end
utilise	use

And moving from sentences like this:

The financial information by business unit provided on pages *xx* to *yy* of these financial statements provides additional voluntary disclosure which the Company considers useful to the users of the financial statements.

To ones more like this:

While we're not required to report the financial information by business unit on pages *xx-yy*, we choose to do this because we believe it may be useful to readers.

---

3 Be concise and to the point

Concise writing shows clear thinking. It also shows respect for report readers (and their time) to put information across in the clearest, simplest terms. It makes it easier for people to skim pages and find the information they're looking for. And it gives messages a more confident tone.

Where things are heavily regulated, such as around remuneration, help readers see the main points by giving them an up-front summary before diving into the detail.

Move from sentences like this:

In support of its internal audit function, the Company utilises the services of external service providers. The function has a policy that addresses conflicts of interest in relation to engagements of the service provider that are requested by management. The policy complies with the IIA's standards on independence. Certain services are pre-approved under the policy as they are not in conflict with the internal auditor's role. There is a list of prohibited services which may not be undertaken without approval of the head of Group Internal Audit, and guidance on the consideration of services which may give rise to a conflict of interest.

To ones more like this:

When needed, the team brings in external partners to help achieve their goals. We have a clear policy to address any conflicts of interest which complies with the IIA's standards on independence. This includes a list of services which need prior approval from the head of Group Internal Audit.

4 Focus on people, using active verbs

Passive language is distancing and long-winded, and often clouds meaning. It also distances you from responsibility, which is why you often see it creeping into an otherwise well-written report when a company has something difficult to acknowledge, like laying people off. Being clear about who the 'doer' is – and presenting your company as real people – will improve both the tone and readability of your report, and make you appear more human, and thus more believable. People are often nervous about this kind of direct writing, because they think it sounds less professional, and therefore less credible, than convoluted, formal language. The answer's simple: it doesn't – in fact, quite the opposite. Readers are more likely to believe it because it sounds confident and honest.

This means moving from passive phrases like 'a decision has been made' to active ones like 'we've decided'. It means saying 'we', instead of 'the Company' or your company name, unless you need to specify this to be clear.

And it means instead of writing sentences like this:

As a result of a changing customer base refocusing on the growth markets of Latin America, and away from Western Europe, the sales function has been reorganised; further resources have been recruited in Brazil, with a downscaling of resource in Germany.

Writing ones like this:

We now have far more customers in Latin America, a growing market, than in Western Europe. We have therefore restructured our sales team, and have recruited 30 people for our office in Brazil. Unfortunately, it also means we've had to lose 20 good people from our office in Germany, and our HR team is offering a programme to help them find other jobs.

None of this is radical stuff – these are good basic writing techniques. But many annual reports do the exact opposite, and as a result they feel unclear and inaccessible. If you do nothing else, apply these four techniques to the writing of your annual report – your readers will thank you for it.

Be smart with your design

So far, we've talked mostly about reading reports, and about the kind of language that facilitates this. But finding the right visual approach for your message is just as important. After all, no one reads a report cover to cover – they flick through, looking for information. So things need to be easy to find, and key messages need to jump out. Enter the designer.

'Good report design is a real art form,' as one FTSE 100 company secretary puts it, 'and helps bring the annual report to life.' Design illuminates content, amplifies messages and helps the reader through. This marriage of design and content can only happen when designers and writers work together, so that the design enhances the content, and vice versa.

This is why it's so crucial that designers and writers get together early on, and work from the same brief. In this way, designs can be created with an understanding of the story that needs to be told (the content plan), and content can be written with an understanding of how it will fit the design (thinking about word counts, options for highlighting key messages on a page, and so on).

We like to think of corporate reporting design as turning information into communication. You may not want or feel you need a 'designed' report. But you do need to apply some of the basics of good information design to make sure people can both follow your story and find what they're looking for. Think of your design layout like giving a speech – the principles are similar:

- Make your headlines loud and clear
- Keep key messages short and punchy
- Deliver more detailed information more quietly
- White space is everyone's friend – think of this as pauses in a speech, which give people time to take in information.

Like a good speaker, a good design layout will guide readers seamlessly through a report at a pace that allows people to take everything on board. This means an unambiguous hierarchy of information, so readers know exactly where they are and what they're being told. It means using visuals like infographics or photography to enhance the message, but not overdoing the graphic bells and whistles just for the sake of it.

Good visual design is, of course, fundamental to engaging the reader. This is where imagination and originality will make your report stand out, grab people's attention and make them want to read on. A FTSE 250 company secretary sums it up: 'Too many annual reports are just words on a page and don't bring the business to life. They need to look good!'

Produce your report well

So how do we get those pages, that story, into their hands, and make sure that the production does justice to all your hard work in writing and design?

Over the years there's been a lot of debate over whether annual reports should be printed at all, whether they should be designed as websites, and so on. Given that annual reports are long-form content and likely to stay that way, then the printed document – or at least the PDF that can be printed off – is also here to stay. The requirement to print the annual report for shareholders who want it shows no sign of disappearing either, and many companies say that they like having printed copies of the annual report to give to employees or other stakeholders, particularly if it's beautifully produced. It's back to that sense of engagement. So, if you've gone to all the hard work of creating something that looks great, make sure the final step in the production process – print – doesn't let you down. See Chapter 3, pages 146-148, for tips on managing print production.

But most readers will access the annual report online. So how do you help them find it, and get the information they want from it? The days of producing full HTML report microsites that replicate to the letter the content of the print-ready PDF have also come and gone – not least because they didn't work and people didn't use them.

Many companies just publish the PDF, but if you want to make more of a fanfare at its publication, then you can include an annual review or summary section embedded in your website that lets skim readers get a sense of the story and the messages without having to download the PDF. The important thing is to make sure the content works for the channel – and to make sure that you've properly planned it into the project.

There is, however, a much bigger opportunity here. After all, you've gone to the effort and cost of thinking about, planning, writing, designing and producing your corporate story, and including a wealth of information – how are you going to make the most of it? Chapter 6 has a wider discussion of how you can maximise your investment in reporting by using the annual report story and content as the foundation of all your communications. ■

A!

To recap

When it comes to reporting, 'telling your story' isn't just about words on a page. For reports to be effective for the reader, they have to be well-designed, clearly signposted, and work on a number of levels. People read annual reports in different ways – some dip in and out, some simply skim read, while others read in more depth. A good annual report that serves all its readers and its own purpose of building trust with them needs its design, writing and layout working together to tell a useful and engaging story, and signposting important information.

In summary, to make your report useful and engaging, you need to:
- Have something useful to say (your story of the year) and say it in a way that can be understood
- Take the time to create a thorough brief to set the direction and voice, and give the entire reporting team a shared view of 'what good looks like'
- Start with your story and fill in the tick-box bits afterwards
- Be purposeful and concise – what you leave out is just as important as what you put in

→

- Establish a voice that's right for your brand and reporting audience and fight to keep this consistent through the many rounds of reviews and revisions
- Consistently apply basic good writing techniques to open up your report to your readers
- Get your designer and writer/editor (whether internal or external) working together from the start so that your words and visuals enhance each other
- Remember that many people download the annual report as a PDF online, so your design should take that into account
- Remind contributors and writers that the report must be fair, balanced and understandable
- Remember that all this guidance isn't just for the strategic report – the governance report and financial statements have their readers too and they deserve similar consideration!
- Don't underestimate the power of a good writer or editor in sharpening your message – so make sure you have one person who can exert editorial control over what is a collaborative document.

Spotlight on small cap companies

Interview with Rachael Matzopoulos, former Deputy Company Secretary, The Vitec Group plc

Well known in reporting circles for the quality of its annual reports, The Vitec Group plc is a small cap listed on the London Stock Exchange that supplies equipment and services to the image capture and content creation market – broadcasters, film studios, independents. Rachael Matzopoulos, Deputy Company Secretary, talked to us about how they see reporting, its benefits and challenges.

Q – How valuable is reporting for small caps?
A – Done well, it's hugely valuable. A small cap has to work much harder to attract investors, generate positive publicity and get capital than a FTSE 100, say, while we don't have the time and money that they do to spend on other collateral. So the annual report, which we are required to produce, becomes even more important.

Q – How do you use your annual report?
A – Aside from the core demographic of investors, we use it widely as a comms and marketing tool to engage with all our stakeholders. We've acquired many small businesses in the last few years, dotted around the world, and we send copies to all of them. Given how dispersed

we are, and how difficult it is to help employees feel connected to the Group, the annual report is really important for educating them about the company, and helping them understand and value being part of it. On a practical level it's been very helpful in promoting our employee share ownership scheme! And, our local salespeople find it useful as collateral with customers to show who we are as a global Group.

Q – You're known for the quality of your reporting – how do you do it?
A – When I started here some years ago, the annual report was more of a compliance document, albeit an award-winning one. That's developed over the years and, after hiring a director of communications, we discovered the 'why' of reporting – to tell our story in our own words, and really use the report to communicate and build a relationship with stakeholders. When you find your 'why', then you do it better. We now see the report as an annual opportunity to review who we are, what we do and how we present ourselves.

Q – What are the challenges?
A – In some ways it's the same as any other company – with increasing regulation, ever larger annual reports are just more and more words on a page; people don't bring their business to life. We have an in-built advantage of being an image company, which means we've always been able to make our report look good! But we still use an agency, whose skills are really important in bringing our story to life. And you need to write what you want, explaining your company in your own words, not just follow the regulations.

Being a small company, there is of course the resource challenge – we're a small team and there's a lot to do. But that can also be a benefit – it's much more streamlined to manage, with a small number of knowledgeable and qualified people providing information.

> ❝ *The report is an annual opportunity to review who we are, what we do and how we present ourselves.* ❞

Q – What advice would you give a fellow small cap looking to improve their reporting?

A – Company secretaries have many skills, but in general we're fundamentally compliance-driven, not creative people! We're very good at providing the project management support, and of course we have to make sure the report is compliant, but the core messaging in the strategic report should be owned by comms. You therefore need a strong partnership between comms/IR (whoever owns the story) and co sec to make sure the annual report is story-driven, while ticking the boxes. Of course, the middle sections comprising governance and remuneration remain firmly under our remit for drafting and bringing to life.

Having one person editing the front section – in our case the comms director – who knows and can write the company story is very beneficial. You don't have the logistical and consistency problems of the annual report, the investor presentation, results announcement and so forth all being done by different people. And you also don't have the problems of very different people writing sections in different styles and tones, and the issues of repetition and conflicting statements.

> ❝ *Whoever's writing has to understand how to write to fit a design concept, so that the report is a coherent whole.* ❞

We still have many contributors, of course, and getting them on side is very important. In our case they're mostly quite senior people, heads of businesses, and they're involved in the planning and briefing process so they feel ownership while understanding what the report has to achieve and why it has to be written centrally. The other key thing is to start early, which gives you the time to get people's buy-in.

When it comes to managing changes and proofs, we've got much better at keeping documents in Word for longer. This is important because by the time they do get into the designed version, they're 90% there, which means fewer amends. But to do that, whoever's writing has to understand how to write to fit a design concept, so that the report is a coherent whole.

Q – What's your view on using design agencies?
A – We use an agency to manage design and typesetting, and their input is invaluable to the overall production of the report. Having a strong relationship with an open communication style is paramount to getting the best out of any agency. It's not easy for them to manage their workload with our demanding priorities of turning proofs all the time. It's not uncommon to be speaking to them multiple times a day towards publication date – so you need to get on!

Q – What benefits have you seen since improving your reporting?
A – It's really contributed enormously to our business – our engagement with our stakeholders has improved massively. Our employees, for example, clearly feel more part of the group, and it's made it easier to hire good people. Also, our customers now recognise the different brands within the group, while our investors have told us they understand our investment proposition and story better. ■

WHAT ARE 'SMALL CAP' OR 'SMALLER QUOTED COMPANIES'?

In the UK, companies are listed either on the London Stock Exchange (the main market), which has two key types of listing, premium and standard, or the Alternative Investment Market (AIM). AIM was set up for companies that had outgrown their initial external capital, often provided by friends and family, or 'angel' investors, but were not yet of a size to warrant the costs and resources needed to maintain a main market listing. AIM, therefore, plays an important role in the funding environment by bridging this gap for smaller, growing companies and lowering the barriers to listing, thus encouraging growth.

Companies are considered to be large, mid or small cap based on their market capitalisation (that is, their overall value based on their share price). In terms of size, companies listed on the London Stock Exchange are generally sub-divided.

As a general rule, large caps are considered to be those included in the FTSE 100 Index; mid caps those in the FTSE 250; and small caps those which fall below this threshold. It is only with a premium listing that a company can be eligible to be included in the FTSE indices, and standard listed companies are generally classified as small caps.

Small caps listed on the main market and AIM-quoted companies are often referred to collectively as 'smaller quoted companies', although there are important differences between the regulatory, governance and reporting requirements both within the main market, depending on the type of listing, and between the main market and AIM.

DO SMALL CAP COMPANIES' REPORTING REQUIREMENTS DIFFER FROM THOSE OF LARGER COMPANIES?

It depends where they are listed and on the type of listing; the related reporting requirements apply regardless of a company's size. Companies with a premium listing must meet both the UK Listing Authority's listing rules, which are more onerous than the minimum EU requirements, and the UK's highest standards of regulation and corporate governance. Those with a standard listing only have to meet EU minimum requirements and do not have to comply with the UK Corporate Governance Code.

The AIM market has a simplified regulatory and reporting environment specifically designed for the needs of small and emerging companies. Unlike other listed small caps, AIM companies are not subject to the UK Listing Authority listing rules, but instead must comply with the less onerous AIM rules, which include certain mandatory reporting requirements including the use of International Financial Reporting Standards (IFRS). AIM-listed companies do not have to follow the UK Corporate Governance Code; instead, AIM rules require them to give details on a website of a recognised code of corporate governance the Board has decided to apply, together with details of how the company has complied with that code and details of any non-compliance. AIM companies are encouraged to adhere to the Quoted Companies Alliance (QCA) Guidelines, which have some similarities to the Code but are tailored to the needs of growth companies and their investors. In practice, most do.

AIM companies also have longer to announce – annual reports must be published within six months of the year end, and half-year reports within three months of the end of the period.

HOW WELL DO SMALL CAP COMPANIES REPORT?

As with larger companies, the picture is mixed. Some companies see huge value in reporting and do it well; others hold the view that no one reads them so it's a waste of time. Perhaps because of their smaller size, smaller companies tend to be scrutinised less, and this could explain why policy-makers have, over the last five years or so, focused on improving their quality.

In response to this concern, the FRC carried out a review in 2015, 'Improving the Quality of Reporting by Smaller Listed and AIM Quoted Companies', which found that, 'whilst the system of financial reporting is not fundamentally flawed, there is a higher incidence of poorer quality annual reports by smaller quoted companies than by their larger counterparts'. Since then, it has cited improvements, but nonetheless their follow-up report of 2018 maintained this view – 'there is still clear scope for further improvement in reporting by smaller companies'.

This perhaps paints rather too gloomy a picture – there is much good reporting amongst small cap firms, perhaps because they have more latitude to be creative in their response to reporting regulation, and there's less of it, so it's easier to produce an engaging report.

WHAT ARE THE BENEFITS AND CHALLENGES OF GOOD REPORTING FOR SMALL CAPS?

The benefits and challenges are the same as they are for larger companies, but in a sense magnified. Smaller companies, by virtue of their size, will have less to cover in their reports, which should make them easier to prepare. But they also tend to have fewer people to manage and produce them, and less budget to pay for external expertise, which can make it more burdensome. (Although having fewer people involved can be an advantage since it means fewer voices trying to be heard, making a more consistent message and tone of voice easier to achieve.) On the other hand, because small cap companies tend to get less media coverage, and fewer analysts' reports, the annual report has the potential to be an even more important document that can affect investment, ratings and lending decisions.

CHAPTER 5

Them = Us

How to work well with your agency

by Claire Bodanis

Questions this chapter will answer

- What is a reporting agency?
- What's the essence of a good agency/client relationship?
- What should you expect from your agency – and what should they expect from you?
- How should I approach choosing an agency?

Not everyone works with corporate reporting agencies, but most medium and large companies do. If you don't, you might it find it useful to read this anyway, to see how the right agency might be able to help you produce a better report, or make your process easier. If you do, you may already feel you have the perfect relationship, so by all means move to Chapter 6! If you have an agency but you feel the relationship could be better, then this chapter should help.

THE NICEST THING A CLIENT EVER SAID TO ME WAS 'I couldn't imagine doing this report without you.' As an agency person for my whole career, this sums up how the very best working relationship between agency and client should feel. And it means a lot because this client is also someone I learn from and respect enormously. Our relationship is a true partnership of mutual understanding and trust, a theme which has resonated throughout the conversations I've had with the companies and agencies who've contributed their views to this chapter.

The importance of this kind of relationship – a partnership – can, of course, be said of any client/agency relationship. But it's particularly crucial when it comes to reporting, since the annual report is such a challenging, critical and high-profile project. And, unlike almost any other corporate publication, it has to be approved by the Board and produced on a specific date, so the ultimate deadline cannot shift.

As the client, you need to feel that the team you're working with really know what they're doing, and that you can rely on them completely when the inevitable problems arise. 'You need people who care like we do – who want it to be good. Some people don't, and we don't stay working with people like that,' comments a FTSE 100 company secretary in the retail sector. Similarly, the best clients respect what their agencies do and care about getting it right, not just getting it done. As Miles Wratten from design agency Emperor says: 'A great client is one whose first thought is to call us because they have confidence that we will listen, understand, challenge or advise, because there is absolute trust that together we will find the right solution.'

So what makes a relationship of absolute mutual understanding and trust? It's very much an individual thing. In the same way that, for your report to be done well it needs to be unique to you, so too will your best agency relationship be unique to you. Companies often ask which is the best reporting agency, but the truth is there isn't one best agency or agency team who would work brilliantly with everyone – just like there is no one best client either.

Good agencies are partners, not suppliers
Why is that? Because it's all about people. When you work with an agency on corporate reporting, you're not paying for a product from a supplier. You're buying specific people's expertise, time and commitment – in other words, paying for a partner. While everyone wants to work with good people, it goes further than that – the people you personally get on best with, and trust most, may well be different from the people someone else does. A FTSE 250 company secretary from the property sector sums it up: 'You need someone who thinks like you.'

Like any relationship, a client/agency one needs work and will take time to establish. 'You need the right creative agency on board – someone who understands you and your values. But even when you get a good one, it can take two or three years to get the best value from them – you've got to let them get to know the business,' explains a FTSE 100 company secretary from the financial sector.

Annual reports are, of course, created by teams on both sides, not by individuals, and you can't expect everyone to get on equally. Often the best client/agency relationships are ones where particular individuals from each side get on well with each other, even if not everyone does. What holds the team together though, despite personality differences, is the belief that what you're doing matters. 'It's about all of us being in it together and being one team,' says a property sector FTSE 250 company secretary. 'We won an award one year, and it was the whole team, not just the company or the agency.'

So what makes a relationship of mutual understanding and trust between client and agency? There are some basic principles of being a good partner that apply to anyone, as we discuss below. Beyond that, it's about working with people you respect and like. After all, you may have to spend 16-hour days with each other, or even work through the night if something unexpected like a major transaction happens at the last minute – so you want it to be as enjoyable as possible. One client's comment that I've always appreciated is: 'I knew reporting was hard work, but I never knew it could be fun!'

> **WHAT IS A CORPORATE REPORTING AGENCY?**
>
> There is no one type of corporate reporting agency. Many agencies offer corporate reporting services – from consulting on report content and communications strategy, to writing, design, typesetting, print management, and digital and other production services. They may offer all or just some of these, and other communications services too. Agencies may call themselves all sorts of things – corporate reporting agencies, writing agencies, design agencies, branding agencies, digital agencies, typesetting/production agencies – or, if they cover everything, corporate communications agencies (or consultancies). It doesn't really matter – as long as the agency or agencies you choose offer the services and support you need through people you want to work with.

The principles of a good client/agency partnership
Create a single team with the right expertise
Many clients, when they want help from a reporting agency, think about it as 'getting the designers in', because few companies these days have in-house design teams. And those that do may still outsource reporting because annual report design is such a specialist skill. But most agencies offer a much wider spectrum of skills and expertise across consulting, writing, design, project management and production, so it's worth thinking properly about what you can do yourself, and where you need external help.

Let your agency fill your gaps
In line with the 'one team' principle, a good agency can look at the whole project with you, work out where you have gaps and come up with a plan of how to fill them. Of course, not all agencies do everything, but, if you

can't find a particular skill from people in your own network – writing, project management, for example – your agency is a good place to start.

In practice, large companies may well have more than one agency working together on their report. Typically, this will be a design agency, which also tends to manage production, and perhaps a writing agency, which may also help with the internal content management process. If the report is an enormous one, you may have a specialist typesetter as well. And, of course, if there's a digital element beyond publishing the report as a PDF on your website, then the reporting and digital agencies will also have to work together (if they aren't already one and the same).

Managing more than one agency
So how to manage all these people? It's no different from working with just one agency, or even no agency. Everyone working on the report should feel part of a single team. In practice this can be difficult, because agencies can get territorial, particularly if there are overlaps in what each can offer. So it's essential that you, as the client and ultimate owner of the project, are absolutely clear about what you expect from each person or agency and how you expect them to work together. And, that you reassure each party that you value their contribution, so they don't need to worry about being undercut by someone else.

Feeling like a team
Creating a single team is about more than just expertise or the practical side of who's doing what. It's about feeling like you're all in it together and aiming for the same goal. 'Successful agency relationships are ones where the agency truly feels part of the internal team, where you're aligned to the same goals and committed to working together to achieve the same outcome,' says a FTSE 250 communications director from the financial sector. 'This sort of relationship is rare, but it's worth holding out for.'

Develop a process that works for everyone
The mistake people often make is to assume that there's one single perfect process for corporate reporting. This conjures up an image of a series of tasks to be ticked off that will result in a successful report. Tasks and milestones are of course essential, but the process is really about what everyone, both within the core project team and in the wider

company, needs to do between those milestones, and how the project team is going to get them to do it. You'll find a wider discussion of process and project management in Chapter 3; here we talk specifically about it in the context of working with an agency.

Manage people, not things
Like all good project management, managing a reporting project well is about managing people, not tasks. And that's why, like everything else in reporting, the specific ways of working a particular team prefers will be unique to them. 'I've managed reports in a number of different companies now, and every process is different, because the personalities (especially of senior people!) are different,' says a FTSE 100 annual report project manager, pharma sector. 'The best agencies really understand that and fit round it, rather than trying to get us to fit into a pre-determined process.'

The proof of this is what can happen when a new person takes over running what is essentially the same project in a different year – as can happen in reporting when a company secretary moves on and a new one joins. While the milestones of the project are the same each year, the 'doings' between the milestones can change hugely because of the way he or she likes to work. So it's really important that you spend enough time at the start of the project going through every bit of the process together and agreeing how things are going to get done. And, as the project progresses, that you continue to do this at key stages as things change. A good agency will be creative in thinking about how to accommodate a client's internal team and requirements, while a good client will understand exactly what the agency team members are doing and accommodate them, too. They'll also challenge each other's assumptions, so that the process is truly the right one for everyone – not just 'because we've always done it like that'. (More on challenging each other below.)

If you're new to reporting, it may be helpful to have an idea of what tasks an agency's creative process covers.

THE STAGES OF PRODUCING AN ANNUAL REPORT

These are the typical stages for a report to be done well. Who's doing what will depend on what resources you have in-house and how much you outsource.

Stage 1 – project planning and briefing

- Plan the project – who's doing what and when (including critical milestones and sign-off requirements)
- Develop the brief – one of the most critical stages of the process (see Chapter 4, pages 169-172 for what a creative brief should cover); make sure it includes channels and detailed online requirements

Stage 2 – content planning

- Review regulatory requirements and implications for content
- Carry out interviews and gather content from internal experts
- Draft the company story and plan the content structure

Stage 3 – creative concepts

- Develop design concepts (visual and verbal) based on the creative brief, company story and content structure. The first stage would typically be a couple of concepts showing key pages of the report – enough to show how it would work
- Choose a concept and develop the design to cover the whole report
- Define word counts for sections/pages

Stage 4 – writing and design

- Draft copy for all sections in Word – an iterative process that involves the writer working with internal content owners, while also consulting the designer to make sure that the visual and verbal will work together in the final document
- Sign off design and hand over to production to create artwork templates
- Commission photography/illustration if needed

Stage 5 – typesetting and artwork

- Set up the artwork file from approved design templates
- Create the first proof from full draft of copy supplied (copy should be as full and final as possible to minimise amends)
- Review copy and design together in the first proof and rework design/copy parts as necessary to ensure that the right messages come through clearly – this may involve tweaking elements of the design or editing some text
- If you're using an electronic system to edit the words directly in the design files (such as CtrlPrint), make sure users have training or refresher training

Stage 6 – proofing and amends

- Review and edit the proofs – you should be able to complete a report with at most four proofs plus the final document ready for publication
- Include a 'page turn' with content owners and agency team members at each proof – a useful way of checking for quality and consistency, and that the document is a coherent whole
- Have a full editorial read – the best way to see if a report reads well is to read it aloud – this involves editors/contributors doing this in pairs with other colleagues or writers
- Do the technical proofread(s) – done by professional proofreaders, this read looks for inconsistencies, typos, accuracy of cross-references and so forth

Stage 7 – sign-off, print* and publication

- Print process – scatter proof (included here for ease of understanding, although in practical terms this happens earlier in the process, during typesetting and artwork)
- Print process – book proof (ditto)
- Final client and agency review
- Client sign-off – includes auditor and Board sign-off
- Agency prepares final files for print and online publication (there should be no changes to the content after the Board and auditors have signed off, unless approved by the auditors)
- Print process – pass on press
- Interactive PDF/online publication
- Printing and distribution
- Creation and filing of ESEF version

For an explanation of the print process, please see Chapter 3, page 146.

DRAFT OR PROOF?

In reporting terminology, a draft is a Word document and a proof is a designed document (typically a PDF). A report will usually go through a number of drafts in Word, with contributors making changes as tracked changes/comments, before the designers create the first proof. This is because it's easier, cheaper and more efficient to edit in Word than to edit the designed proof.[1] But it is important that people understand the difference, and what the words will look like once they're in the designed format.

---

1 This applies even when you are using an editing system such as CtrlPrint which allows you to edit the InDesign files, because any proof you create by editing the text will still need 'tidying' by your designers.

Support and challenge each other to do it well

'Because we've always done it like that' is a frequent refrain in corporate reporting – sometimes for the process, but more often for the content of the report. If we could ban just one thing from reporting, it would be this as a reason for doing anything. People cling to it because it feels safe – they assume that, if something was like that in previous years and the report was approved, then it must be OK. It's this approach, however, that is anathema to good reporting – as many of our interviewees attest. It results in longer and ever more impenetrable reports, and gives credence to the view that reporting is a waste of time. If you don't know why something is in your annual report, it simply shouldn't be there, as our lawyers note on page 61.

This is where a good agency can be hugely helpful – and a good client is one who will listen and be prepared to debate their questions, a theme that came through from almost everyone we talked to. As one FTSE 100 reporting manager in the food and beverage sector says: 'You need an agency you can learn from – reporting is too complex to have a yes-man.' But you've also got to get the balance right, as noted by Dean Radley, from agency Radley Yeldar: 'Too much push can become frustrating for the client, not enough and you can miss a vital opportunity to improve the report.'

Similarly, agencies need to take feedback well, and interrogate it so that they understand why something needs to change and can come up with the right solution. He continues: 'Feedback can be ambiguous. So, for example "I don't like the design" doesn't tell you anything. You need to know why it's not working, so you can reach a better outcome more quickly and accurately.'

The ability to discuss, question, challenge in good faith – all the elements of a good partnership – are essential for good reporting. Sallie Pilot from agency Black Sun sums up a common agency view: 'The key thing we look for in our clients is ambition to embrace the spirit of good reporting as part of the broader stakeholder communications suite. We place a focus on content and strategy first, ensuring that we understand the challenges and opportunities that our clients face. The hallmark of a great client is one who is willing to embrace those challenges and who shares our ambition to deliver creative and messaging that has real impact.'

> **UNDERSTANDING YOUR STORY**
>
> See also the briefing section in Chapter 4.
>
> To get the best from your agency – whether they're writing, designing or both – it's essential that you enable them to understand the company story, and that they work hard to do so. Only by really getting under the skin of your company can they properly bring your story to life. A thorough briefing process, in which your agency can ask searching questions of senior management, is at the heart of this. As noted in Chapter 3, it really helps if you get the CEO or CFO involved at the start of the process and include your agency in that meeting. Even half an hour with them will help avoid anything getting lost in translation. Karen Almeida of agency Conran Design Group says: 'A good relationship starts with an appetite for communication and an appreciation of the value that good design can bring to the way businesses tell their stories. Clear briefs, being receptive to new ideas and a willingness to listen all help. And, of course, trust, fairness and a sense of humour! These are the hallmarks of the clients we love working with.'

Be responsive and flexible

Responsiveness is one of the most important factors in a good client/agency relationship – in fact, the lack of it is one of the most frequently cited frustrations companies have with their agencies. 'I want to know I can contact the key people at all times and that they're with me on the journey,' says a FTSE 100 company secretary from the extractive sector. 'My big worry is agencies who overcommit and underdeliver – if your team is doing three other big corporate reports all at the same time it raises questions.' But bear in mind, of course, that agencies' time is money, so if you do want a dedicated resource you'll need to pay for it – more on budgets below.

Being responsive doesn't necessarily mean you have to do something straight away, but, for example, simply acknowledging that you've received a message and that you'll deal with it by the time it's needed.

This means the other side can stop worrying about it. And, if you're running the project, make sure you always have cover, so there's never a hiatus in communication, which can get particularly stressful on critical days. This applies to you as the client as much as to your agency. It's just as important that you are responsive to them, especially during the proofing and amends stages when things are moving at speed. It's not conducive to a partnership relationship to expect your agency to jump on things immediately and be endlessly available if you don't give them the same support in return.

None of this is particularly complicated, but a lack of responsiveness can cause enormous stress and worry, and have a very detrimental effect on the team's morale. After all, if your boss sent you a message, you'd answer pretty quickly – so give the same level of consideration to the rest of the annual report team, who will be working very hard on your behalf.

Clive Bidwell of agency Friend Studio sums it up: 'Communication is the key to a successful client/agency relationship; open, honest, collaborative, frequent and timely. Covering ambitions, progress, challenges and feedback.'

Be creative in accommodating changes
'An agency has to be flexible and responsive, and prepared to tweak things – we're quite demanding!' says one REIT FTSE 250 company secretary. Flexibility is related to responsiveness – both are about how you interact and accommodate each other's needs. Back to the point that reporting is about managing people not tasks – the first rule of reporting project management is that the plan and the schedule will change, and change frequently. The key for both agency and client is to anticipate changes, and be creative in managing them so that they're accommodated without making unreasonable demands of the team.

Understand the implications of what you're asking
Again, this boils down to respect, and understanding each other's role and how long things take. Asking your agency to reflow the chief executive's statement in an hour is probably reasonable if someone's available to do it, and if the new text is the same length. Asking them to lay out the remuneration report again in that time most certainly isn't. A good

agency will be honest about how long things take, and will do their best to accommodate urgent changes. But clients must, in turn, be reasonable and accept that some things just aren't possible.

The more your internal team understands how things work, the less likely you are as project manager to be asked by them for the impossible. This is especially important when it comes to senior management and the Board, because of their authority to make changes. 'You need to know the end-to-end process so that you know what you can and can't change,' offers a FTSE 100 company secretary from the financial sector. 'It's very useful in Board meetings when they get a big idea late on and want to change something – you can explain why they can't!'

Be open and fair about time and cost
The basic economics of an agency's budget are the team's time plus bought-in expenses (such as printing, travel etc). At the outset, a good agency will be clear about the daily or hourly rates for each role, the time they expect each person to spend at each stage of the project, and the page rates for typesetting and production if those are charged by page. They will also tell you if there are likely to be expenses, and set a budget for those too. It's perfectly reasonable for an agency to charge a management or handling fee, particularly for external services like photography or print, because there's often quite a lot of work involved in organising these things. But the expense itself should be charged at cost, with the management fee separated out, rather than a blanket mark-up being charged.

So far, so obvious. But it's really all about the detail. To create a budget, agencies have to work out to the hour what each person is going to be doing. This is generally quite easy if you've done the project together before, since they'll know how long things actually take. But when you work together for the first time, there can be a lot of guesswork. And a big problem for client/agency relationships is the budgetary implication of what a client is asking for. The more you understand about what each other is doing, and why things take the time that they do, the less scope there is for suspicion and mistrust over what you're being charged for.

Spend time properly discussing the budget
For that reason, the best way to create a budget is to have a detailed discussion about exactly what everyone will be doing, and who's going to be managing what and when, so the agency can estimate properly what you need them to do. And make sure you have a thorough discussion about amends and how they'll be managed (see box on page 206 – know the cost of amends). Too many clients complain about not understanding what they're being charged for – so, if anything isn't clear, ask!

Nonetheless, annual report projects always change, which is why you also need contingencies at every stage of your budget. And a good agency will give you regular budget updates so you know where you are and whether you need to dip into your contingency pot; in this way you'll be able to act before going over budget, rather than having to deal with it afterwards. Internally, having a contingency is also a good tactic because, while it's often hard to go back and ask for more money if you've underbudgeted, it's similarly useful to have budget left over at the end, either to put back in the pot, or to use for something else. 'We really value the absolute accuracy and honesty of our agency in recording their hours and letting us know where we are on budget – it reflects the integrity that's a fundamental quality of our relationship', says a large-cap company reporting manager. 'And, since we have the full amount accounted for in the corporate budget, we often use any overage with them on other projects!'

Don't expect a fixed cost – allow for changes
Companies – particularly procurement departments – often want a fixed cost. This is an entirely unfair expectation. Fixed costs work for fixed things, and annual report projects are not fixed things. For example, if you've asked your agency to estimate production costs for, say, a 120-page report, and it comes in at 200 pages, then it's going to cost more. Similarly, if you were planning to collate and check amends from contributors on your draft copy yourself, and then need your copywriter or agency project manager to do it, then it's only fair that you pay for that time. But companies need to set budgets and have them approved in advance – so how to square the circle? The way round this is to make sure that the budget you get approval for has anticipated every possible contingency, as discussed above. That way you have the flexibility to cover changes.

A good agency will help you here, because they'll tell you if what you're asking for goes beyond the scope of what you've agreed. But when you're in the thick of it and things are moving quickly, even the best agency project manager might forget, so do be reasonable. The biggest contributors to annual report budgets overrunning are management issues and miscommunication over who's doing what and when. By respecting the process and making sure everyone does what they've signed up for, the budget becomes easier to stick to.

This is where a good brief and project plan, agreed at the start, come in. The brief lays out the direction for the content, messaging and structure of the annual report, and summarises logistics, while the detailed plan is key for both process and people. You should also think about what your priorities are for your budget – different companies will spend the same pot of money in different ways, depending on what their priorities are. By discussing these in detail and agreeing them at the start, you can make sure your budget matches your aims, and that you're all starting off with the same expectations. For more on what goes into a brief, see pages 169-172, and for more on planning, see pages 124-127.

> **KNOW THE COST OF AMENDS**
>
> A frequent cause of disagreement between agency and client is the cost of amends, which generally results from mismatched expectations. Now that software packages are available that allow non-designers (and non-editors, who may introduce errors by not following their own house style) to edit copy straight into the design files, some clients believe that the cost of amends should be almost nothing. But in reality there's still a lot to do to the files to tidy them up once a client has finished editing. In principle, it's possible for there to be no amends if the copy going to the agency for typesetting has been signed off; in practice this never happens because things always change. Unwary clients can be caught out by an unscrupulous agency artificially reducing the budget by hiding 'amends will be charged by the hour/page' in the small print, rather than highlighting the need for an amends allowance. The solution is easy: as part of the budget discussion, have a thorough and open conversation about the process for amends and the likely cost, then set a realistic budget. And, as the project progresses through proof stages, keep on top of how much you've spent.

Pay your agency on time
A final point on budgets – in most client/agency relationships, the economic balance of power is hugely in a client's favour, because they tend to be much bigger. And, annual report projects may well represent a large percentage of an agency's turnover, particularly if the agency is small, and they often involve freelances who may have to wait to be paid until the client has paid their agency's bill. So it's essential for a good relationship that clients pay their agencies on time. It is fair and reasonable for an agency to invoice a large percentage of the project up front, and then at stages throughout, to keep their cash flow going. And clients should ensure that they set up the payment system at their end speedily so there's no delay in their agency – and sometimes individual team members – getting paid.

Choosing an agency

For small companies and teams who tend to have more autonomy, appointing an agency is often easier than it is for large companies with complex procurement processes. In such companies, the annual report, due to its size and cost, often has to be put out to tender at least every four years, if not every three. Although clients who love their agencies will often do their best to get around such a directive if they really don't want to change.

What should you ask for in a pitch?
What a pitch should involve is a much-debated subject. But if you think logically, what you ask agencies to prepare should demonstrate the qualities, skills and expertise you're looking for. So think about what you're going to base your decision on and design your tender around that.

> **A TIP:**
> Agencies tend to send senior people and their best presenters to meet new clients. Make sure the people you meet will really be working on your project.

Creative pitches – an unfair waste of time and money
For those new to this, a 'creative pitch' is one where you ask the agencies pitching to present new design work for your annual report to your specification. There are different schools of thought on this, but in my view, creative pitching is an unfair, counter-productive exercise that sets the client/agency relationship up on entirely the wrong footing. This is because:

- You should be able to judge the quality of an agency's design work by work they've done for others – you wouldn't ask a solicitor, say, to give a solution to your problem before you pay them, so why should agencies give their work for free?
- An agency that doesn't know you, that hasn't had a proper briefing discussion, that hasn't prepared the content plan or thought through your story – that hasn't gone through stages 1 and 2 of the annual report process set out on page 198, in fact – cannot design your annual report properly. So you'd be choosing your agency based on luck in designing something you like the look of, not on what will necessarily be right.
- Quite reasonably, the winning agency may try to recoup their investment in the pitch by using the design work they created for it for your project too, rather than starting from scratch, so the resulting work is unlikely to be as good as if they'd been able to follow the process properly.

Some large companies do try to be fair by paying for a creative pitch, but a) the money tends to be far less than the true cost of doing it, and b) the problem of creating designs without going through the proper stages of briefing and content planning remains.

Advice for a thorough and fair tender process
Planning the tender
- Before you start, think hard about what you're looking for and why, and make this the basis for all decisions.
- Design your tender around what you're looking for, not just what people typically ask for, and make sure it's a good use of everyone's time.

Creating the shortlist
- Get recommendations from your network and take up references before inviting people to tender – there's nothing like personal experience of working with others. Ask why they'd recommend an agency – and make sure this fits what you're looking for.
- Pitching is time-consuming and expensive for agencies, so only invite ones who really stand a chance. It's better to invite fewer than waste the time of an agency that's been asked just to make up some mythical number.
- Similarly, only invite your incumbent agency if they genuinely stand a chance. If you know you're going to switch agency, then don't ask them; it simply isn't fair.
- Before confirming the shortlist, you should also give agencies a sense of what your budget is, so that they know whether or not they're likely to meet it. It's frustrating for both client and agency if, at the end of the process, it turns out that the best agency is just too expensive. This is a controversial point – companies rarely want to give budgets because they feel that agencies will quote to that figure, even if they don't need it. However, it comes back to the central point about this chapter, which is about trust. If there is absolute openness from the agencies about what their rates are, and how many hours they're going to be spending on each thing, then companies can see whether they think what's being quoted for is reasonable. And if companies start by refusing to tell their agencies what their budget is, then it doesn't set the relationship off on a very open footing.
- It's not unheard of for clients to use a pitch to window-shop for good ideas, which they then take to cheaper agencies. This is simply unethical and shouldn't be done. Companies that do this kind of thing soon get found out, and will find that good agencies won't want to work with them.

Managing the process
- Pitching needs your time if you're to get it right. You're asking a lot from agencies, so make sure you give them enough of your time to prepare properly, and be available for questions beforehand, ideally in person. A face-to-face meeting does a lot for both sides in understanding whether they're likely to get on.
- Make your decision as quickly as possible, and inform everyone who took part.
- Give full and honest feedback to the winner and the losers – it's useful for both. ∎

> *You want someone who listens carefully, takes the time to understand what you really want, and then works with you as a partner to deliver a quality end product. No one wants an agency that thinks they're right regardless of what you say, while an agency that blindly follows what the client wants is no good either. Both need to feel valued and feel free to challenge each other – that's what gets the best results.*
> FTSE 250 corporate relations director, food and beverage sector

A!

To recap

The best client/agency relationships are ones of mutual understanding and trust, and often last for years. Here's how to give yourself the best chance of such a relationship:

- Create a single team ethos for everyone working on the project, both internal and agency teams.
- Remember that managing the project is about managing people, not tasks.
- Give your agency access to the right people, and the time to get to know your business.
- Ban 'because we've always done it like that' as a justification for doing anything – have a logical reason.
- Respond quickly to a request – even if it's just to say 'I'll get back to you soon'.
- Be fair with the budget: agency people's time equals money – so if you ask them to do more, then they should be paid more; and if they do less, you should pay less.
- Go with your instinct and work with people you trust, respect and like.

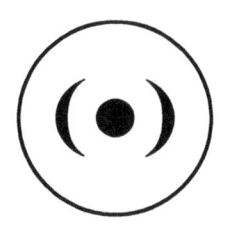

An investor's view 3

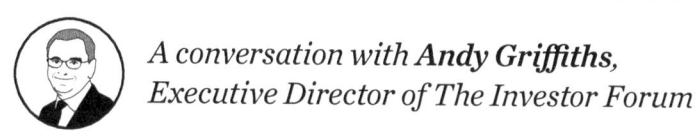

*A conversation with **Andy Griffiths**, Executive Director of The Investor Forum*

Andy, a former equity investor, heads up The Investor Forum, a community interest company set up by institutional investors in UK equities to help build trust between companies and their shareholders by escalating material issues to Boards.

Q – Do investors read annual reports?
A – It depends. The first question is: What is an investor? No two are the same, and no two will agree. On the institutional side, in an investment organisation, you have analysts, generalists, governance people – some will read bits and some won't; no one is likely to read all of a report. And a lot of investors use search engines now to scan and look for phrases – they're not reading reports, unless it's because a company has a problem and they want to find what was said about it. That doesn't mean they don't want companies to produce annual reports – they want to be reassured and know that the information is there – but they don't necessarily read them. When it comes to retail shareholders, you'll get some who read the report, but I doubt they all do – and most are more likely to want a summary.

The problem for producers of annual reports is you've got to write for everyone, without quite knowing who everyone is, what they're looking for, or what they already think of you. And that's before we get into the question of readers beyond the investors.

Q – What's the value in annual reports if not everyone reads them?

A – The requirement reporting makes of companies to tell their story is essential, both for companies and for investors. Companies no longer have total control of their story because of the explosion of information and social media, so they have to work a lot harder to gain credibility and make their version of their story the one that people believe. This also puts a lot of onus on companies to be honest in their annual report. If they're not, no one will believe them because they can get so much other information elsewhere – Glassdoor for the employees' view being the obvious example.

The annual report is your one chance to tell a compelling, integrated story, and if you can do that, you'll draw shareholders to you. If you ignore it, you'll get called out. And the annual report is where this has to be because it's the legally required document. There is of course the consistency point – everything else you say, on your website, in other documents, should be consistent with the annual report, but the report is where it starts.

Q – How could annual reports be improved?

A – You've got to think about the reader. Companies have to throw off the mindset of blindly sticking to the requirements, because these don't help you communicate. In fact, they do the opposite and prevent you writing your own story. Yes, the report has to be compliant, but you can go back and check you've covered everything after you've written it. And starting with last year's answer – last year's report – is not the way to do it. To do reporting well, you have to start by stepping back and thinking – what are we in business for? Why do we do what we do? What does our performance tell us? This isn't easy – it's very hard to define your story, and get a consistent thread across a big range of issues, let alone write it in a meaningful and engaging way. Learning to write an annual report counts as some of the worst months of my life! The readers have no idea what you're going through when you're writing, but it's not their problem. You've got to rise above it and produce something they'll want to read.

Q – How should companies deal with the challenge of storytelling vs ticking the boxes?

A – It's as I said – story first, box ticking second. But I'd like to see a future for reporting in which all the regulatory stuff is dealt with via an EDGAR-type system[1] that contains information or data produced in a consistent format. Alongside this, there'd be a separate 30- to 50-page report where you tell your story, and have the conversation you want, that isn't bound by having to tick a series of potentially unrelated boxes. Whether this will happen any time soon is another question – although one that the FRC's Future of Corporate Reporting Project, will, I hope, address.[2]

Q – What are your thoughts on ESG reporting?

A – People seem to think that ESG reporting is for other stakeholders – employees and suppliers, say – but investors are more and more interested. There's fantastic stuff in some of the other reports or communications companies produce – the sustainability report for example – that doesn't necessarily go into annual reports, and so may get missed by investors, which is a shame. But more broadly, companies have to get comfortable with reporting on these variables that are less in their control than the financial metrics they are used to. If they don't, people will find out about a company's position on an issue from what others say elsewhere via social media or the internet.

The future? I suspect that, in three to five years' time, we'll be wondering why we ever had these segmented conversations, because it'll all join up and ESG reporting will be part of the whole picture. ■

> ❝ *Companies no longer have total control of their story, so they have to work a lot harder to gain credibility and make their version the one that people believe.* ❞

---

[1] The EDGAR (electronic data gathering, analysis and retrieval) system is the US's electronic filing system for company accounts of companies listed on US indices.

[2] See page 96 for a case study on the FRC's Future of Corporate Reporting Project.

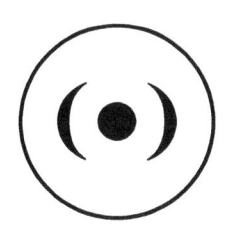

An investor's view 4

*A conversation with **Andrew Ninian**, Director of Stewardship & Corporate Governance at The Investment Association*

The IA is the trade body and industry voice for UK-based investment managers, with members ranging from small independent UK investment firms to Europe-wide and global players. Andrew, an expert on corporate governance, represents the IA's members' interests on all aspects of governance.

Q – What are you looking for in an annual report?
A – We're interested in how companies will deliver long-term value to shareholders, so what matters is a cohesive story. And by story, we mean how do you make money; how are you going to in the future; and what things could occur that might knock you off course. We want to know how all the different aspects of a company's circumstances fit together, particularly the wider stakeholder piece because that's all about long-term value. And, we want to see how the Board is set up to deliver that value. No shareholder is going to read the annual report cover to cover, but these things should still come across.

Accuracy and authenticity are of course important – the facts have got to be true, and the story has to be honest, which means the report has to be well written. I also believe there's a lot of benefit in having to write things down – doing so helps you develop your thinking around an issue, and therefore how you are going to manage it. Looking at that the other way round, a poorly written report gives away a lot about how a company operates. So reading an annual report can be for both positive and negative reasons!

Q – What do you read first?
A – To a large degree I read an annual report for reassurance on key issues. So, the Chairman's statement and CEO's review are very important – not just the content they cover but the tone, and whether they properly acknowledge the challenges they're facing. I'm also keen to see how the company discusses material risks, and the changing nature of risk – not just a bland description but what's really going to have the biggest impact on the company. It's been interesting to see how companies have been reporting on the impacts of Covid-19, and that'll certainly be a focus in the future. This has also thrown a spotlight on auditors' reports which at times can be quite generic, but the heightened focus on going concern because of Covid-19 has made them much more specific to the company. From a governance perspective, I'm of course interested in the governance intro – again, not for whether a company's ticked the boxes of the Code, but for how the Chairman brings to life key questions around governance issues, which are only going to become more important in the current environment.

Q – Tone is an interesting point. Should the whole annual report sound the same?
A – At some level yes, because most of it comes from the company. It should be consistent in story and message. However, the named reports – Chairman, CEO, chairs of committees – should be engaging, and should sound authentic, and by that I mean they should sound as if those individuals have written them. Engaging is difficult to define, but I'd say it's about whether they're saying anything different or meaningful, as opposed to just trotting out the same old stuff year after year. I know some chairs write their own letters, but many don't. And you can tell those who've thought about what they want to say and those who've just had someone write a generic piece for them.

Q – What's your view of breaking up annual reports into different reporting mechanisms?

A – It's a difficult one. The key issue is about materiality: with more and more regulations requiring disclosures in the annual report, they're not as useful for shareholders as they used to be, because they're getting so long, and the important things get drowned out. But on balance I'd probably say there's still merit in it all being in one document – at least you know where to go to find what you're looking for! ■

> ❝ *There's a lot of benefit in having to write things down – doing so helps you develop your thinking around an issue, and therefore how you are going to manage it.* ❞

CHAPTER 6

Sweat the asset

How to get the best return on investment – make the annual report story the foundation of your communications

by Neil Roberts

Questions this chapter will answer

- Why should the annual report be the foundation of your communications?
- What happens if it isn't?
- How do you broaden the annual report process to incorporate wider communications planning?
- Who are my audiences and how do they get their information?
- How important is social media?

I F SOMEONE TELLS YOU ONE STORY about themselves one day, and a different version – or a different story altogether – the next, presenting both as if they were true, which should you believe? Should you believe either? Should you take bits from both and work out what makes most sense, what's most likely to be true? Should you go and ask someone else for their view, just to check? Or, should you just not bother to make the effort, and go and find someone else who'll tell the truth, the same truth, every time you speak to them?

  The basis of trust is consistency. You believe because what you hear, what you see and what you experience add up to the same thing. So with people, as it is with companies. If a company says one thing in one place, and something else – possibly even contradictory – somewhere else, then there is no basis for trust. Even more so if it says something in one place, but what it actually does is something altogether different.

  All companies talk about building trust with their shareholders and wider stakeholders. It's what reporting – and what this book – is all about. Over the last few years, there has been plenty of noise about a 'crisis of trust' in business, and in institutions more widely. This has been exacerbated by the Covid-19 pandemic, as discussed by the 2021 Edelman Trust Barometer, which 'reveals an epidemic of misinformation and widespread mistrust of societal institutions and leaders around the world. Adding to this is a failing trust ecosystem unable to confront the rampant infodemic, leaving the four institutions – business, government, NGOs and media – in an environment of information bankruptcy and a mandate to rebuild trust and chart a new path forward.'

Within this bleak picture there is hope for business, which, with 61% agreeing they trust business to 'do what is right', is 'the most trusted institution among the four studied'. But businesses should not be complacent, because within that, the credibility of CEOs is at 'all-time lows in several countries'.

Many companies fail on trust because what they do doesn't live up to what they say. But time after time, even those that are doing the right thing don't get credit for it, because they often fail when it comes to consistent communications, a consistent message. Why is this? It's not difficult to imagine. If one individual were the only writer, the only spokesperson of a company, then it would be easy.

But the bigger a company gets, the harder consistency becomes, because there are more and more people involved in communicating with external stakeholders, never mind the internal ones. There's the annual report team for one – and we've already discovered how difficult it is even to make the narrative in the annual report itself consistent. Then there may be the global comms or the marketing teams – or both. Not to mention the local or regional comms or marketing teams – or both. And so on. Amongst all these teams, who decides what the message should be? Who signs things off? What are they basing their decision on?

Why the annual report is your best source of truth
The great advantage of the annual report over any other piece of corporate communication is that it covers a wide range of subjects that are of interest to a wide range of stakeholders; it is (or should be) accurate; and it's checked or signed off by just about everyone. Which is why bits of it tend to pop up in all sorts of other areas of communication – the corporate website, internal presentations, marketing documents. Using annual report information is not even low risk for internal teams, it's no risk. However, lifting bits, merging them with other things, and using them in channels for which they weren't written or designed does not produce good or consistent communication, particularly if the annual report hasn't been written or designed that well in the first place.

But within this flight to the annual report as the source of truth lies a powerful idea which, if planned carefully and carried out well, can be the foundation for effective, trustworthy communications with all stakeholders. It is that the story told in the annual report should be the starting point for a comprehensive stakeholder communications plan for the year – and again the following year, and again the year after that.

> **TRUE STORIES, TRUE TALES**
>
> Some people feel uncomfortable with the idea of a company 'story'. It sounds like spin, like you're trying to hide an unpleasant truth. It's true, there's something in the word 'story' that can imply an embroidering of the truth, if not complete fiction. Perhaps it's because as children, we're told not to tell stories, meaning don't lie, and not to tell tales, meaning don't report your pals for harmless naughtiness. The idea of stories and tales is formed in our psyche at an early age with overtones of fiction (or dishonesty) or unlikeable behaviour. And yet it's stories – true ones – that allow us to make sense of the world around us, to connect pieces of data and information together and analyse them to understand their real meaning. As set out in Chapter 1, action + context = story: and it's this that we're aiming for in corporate reporting. Truth of action and truth of context that add up to a true story, an authentic reality that people can believe in.

If you've worked in reporting a long time, it can be difficult to throw off the ingrained feeling that the annual report is no more than the formal document of record, the report from Board to shareholders, even if it has broadened out in the last few years. And, judging by some reports you see today, you'd be forgiven for thinking that this was still the case. However, if you can forget past experience, come to reporting afresh, and pay attention to the principles behind reporting, then the annual report as the source of truth for everything starts to make sense.

Let's look at regulatory creep in a positive light. It's great for those who want to communicate openly and honestly about what their company is doing. The fact that regulators are requiring companies to be far more transparent about their relationships with all stakeholders, and about how they take account of their impacts on society and the planet as well as their financial returns, means that the discussion of all these things should now happen at the most senior level. And, therefore, that the core story told in the annual report should be comprehensive enough to stand as the foundation for a full communications plan.

Get a far better return on your investment
At a more prosaic level, gone are the days of the annual report that's literally just that – a statement of what happened last year. In a good annual report today, you're creating a focused piece of communication that reflects your culture, sets the tone, and explains your business and your ambitions, targets, and strategic vision for at least the next year if not longer. And you're doing it through a process which already involves people from right across the business. Why on earth *wouldn't* you use it? And why *wouldn't* you make sure that the story you've worked so hard to get right reaches as many stakeholders as it can through the channels that they use?

A vast amount of capital goes into the annual report. Money, certainly. Even if you're not paying agencies to help you, you'll doubtless be paying lawyers and auditors, and possibly remuneration and other advisers as well. Then there's your own people's time and effort, which, if expressed financially, would probably dwarf the rest of the budget. And there's the relationship capital both across the business and upwards to senior management and the Board, that can be built or squandered, depending on how well the process is managed. That's a lot to put into a single project if all it does is produce a document that gets read by a handful of people, even if it does tick the essential legal box.

With all this capital going into the annual report, it's a) worth doing well, which is what this book is about, and b) worth making the most of, which is what this chapter is about. Forget for a minute that it's an annual report, a statutory document, and think about what wealth it contains in the form of an accurate, approved story and supporting information that could be used to great effect in other ways.

> ❝ *Why wouldn't you make sure that the story you've worked so hard to get right reaches as many stakeholders as it can through the channels that they use?* ❞

Make the story the foundation of your communications – democratise the process

The idea of using the content in the annual report in other ways isn't new. But, beyond repurposing it by updating facts and figures, stories and pictures on the corporate website, and pulling things out of it for the intranet, that's often as far it gets. And, even when it is used, it's often not very successful because something written for a long-form document doesn't always translate very well into other media.

However, what we're talking about here isn't taking the finished annual report, chopping it up and putting it in other places. And it's not about pouring more money into the annual report format itself to create microsites, or doing a vast print run and sending it to all and sundry. Rather, it's about taking the story being told in the annual report, and writing and producing that same story in different ways to get it in front of the people who should be reading it, on the devices or channels through which they access information. It's about broadening the briefing and story development part of the annual report process such that they become the brief and story for your overall corporate communications plan for the year, rather than just for the annual report – see figure 1.

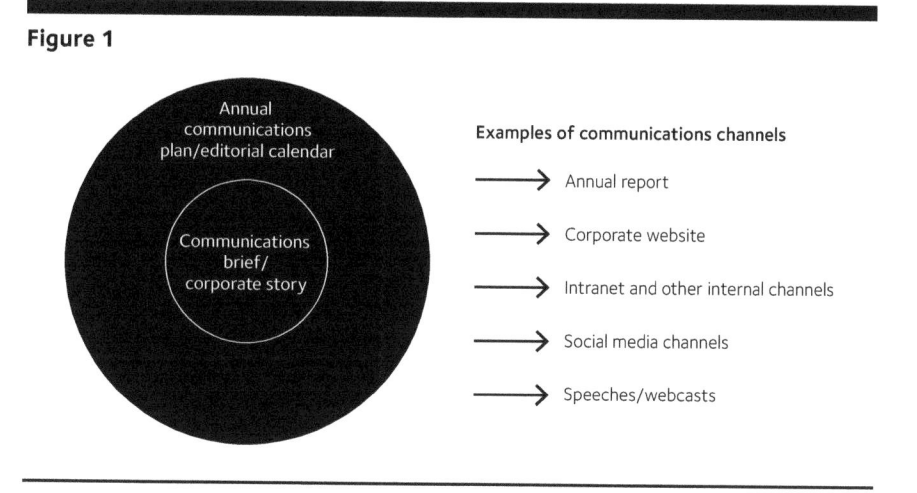

Figure 1

Annual communications plan/editorial calendar

Communications brief/corporate story

Examples of communications channels

⟶ Annual report

⟶ Corporate website

⟶ Intranet and other internal channels

⟶ Social media channels

⟶ Speeches/webcasts

Doing this is about bringing together and involving the right people. 'When I know that the annual report is being planned, I get myself invited to the briefing discussion with the CEO and CFO so that I can get the story to use in my own channels,' comments the digital communications director of a small cap company, who uses the annual report process to find out the corporate story each year and so inform his own communications channels.

How do you broaden the process?
How you democratise the process will be unique to your company. But the principle is straightforward – it's an expansion of the 'single team' principle for getting the annual report done successfully (see Chapters 3 and 5). The leader of every team involved in creating communications of whatever sort for whatever audience should be involved so they know what the company is aiming to achieve and what the story is for the year.

In a small company, with a small internal team, this should be relatively easy. For larger companies it may be more difficult, with different teams responsible for different aspects of communication, marketing, IR, and reporting, and quite often different views of what should be done. If you're responsible for producing the annual report you may well shudder at the idea of making life even more complicated by involving all these other people. But, if approached in the right spirit, it should be possible to build consensus and make this work to everyone's advantage – because after all, it's in everyone's interests to have a consistent message, engagingly told. 'Getting key players all together and all on the same page and in the timescales required when you need to produce an annual report will not be easy,' says a FTSE 100 annual report project manager. 'But that doesn't mean the annual report story should not be the foundation of a company's communications. Even if companies only get part of the way there, it will be a start.'

I may be stating the obvious here, but the following are a few suggestions on how to get started:
- Find out who the full list of people should be and discuss the idea with each of them in turn
- Determine approvals and sign-off processes for the communications brief, plan and corporate story, and then the different channels of communication – this is critical to avoid the whole approach breaking down (see also the guidelines point on page 230 for when communications have to be particularly fast)
- Convene an initial meeting to bring people together to discuss and agree how this new comms planning process will work and feed into each team's annual plan
- Create the overarching communications plan.

Building a communications plan
Again, how you build a company-wide communications plan will be unique to your own company – and you may be doing it already. If not, here are some pointers to help you think about how to build a plan:
- **Know your audiences and channels:** define who your audiences are, what channels they use, how you're going to reach them – and how they're going to reach you (don't forget that this information will be very useful for the stakeholder reporting you have to do in the annual report anyway). And don't guess – you need to conduct research here to be sure of your facts. It'll be worth it in the long run.
- **Create a brief for the corporate comms year as a whole:** the structure of the briefing document (see Chapter 4) can be used for the whole communications plan, with the annual report brief becoming a subset of it. The corporate story, as developed for the annual report with its wide stakeholder reach, will then become the basis for communicating with all your audiences across all channels. Consider questions like: which parts of the story do different people want to know about? What aspects should be developed? How could they be developed?

- **Be creative with your media:** think of all the ways corporate audiences absorb information and find stories. Film, animation, pictures, words. Then match information, channel and audience together. Remember that channel and format may change for the same information, depending on the audience. Take the annual results, for example. Analysts will need the data in black and white as concrete evidence. Employees, however, may simply want to be reassured and inspired for the coming year – so perhaps a CEO video, streamed to all offices, would work better.
- **Establish editorial guidelines based on the story brief, ownership and sign-off of every channel:** remember that, in the case of social media in particular, comms have to be fast, and reactions even faster. In bigger organisations, people don't always have time to ask or approve – so make sure there are clear guidelines.
- **Match your narrative reporting approach to your financial reporting approach with an editorial calendar:** the finance team don't leave it until month 10 before starting to gather the numbers – they are preparing their part of the annual report every month through the month-end process. By establishing an editorial 'month-end process', which is both a calendar of things you want to say during the year and a repository for stories happening in your business or in the wider world that that you want to respond to, you will do two things. You'll ensure that you are sharing content consistently that is 'on message' (and therefore building trust with people that matter), and you'll make your life easier when it comes to gathering stories for the report itself by having a rich repository of content to draw from.

- **Find your eyes and ears:** in large companies in particular, you can't be everywhere, all of the time. So create a team of people on the ground who are your local roving reporters and who'll tell you what's going on, good and bad.
- **Expect change – and use it creatively:** the company story, as told through the annual report, should be your foundation at the start of the year; its principles and key messages won't change. But the essence of good communication is to be responsive to events as they happen. In this context, if you let your principles and key messages be your guide in how to respond, then your communication will indeed be consistent and believable by your stakeholders.

> **A BOTTOM-UP APPROACH IS A GOOD START!**
>
> 'The best we've achieved in any of the large companies I've worked at has been to ensure that some of the key players in creating communications across the business are either key contributors to the annual report, or have the opportunity to review and comment on the report at key stages, so that other communications can be aligned,' says a FTSE 100 reporting manager. 'So it's more of a bottom-up approach. Today, rather than coming together and formulating a comms plan and story with one of the channels being the annual report, in developing the story for the report, we bring in the key players so that they can then tell the right story to their audiences through other channels. We also have a comms lead for the report who ensures that any elements repurposed elsewhere are used accurately and consistently, or are provided in a form that others can use. We also have an editorial board for the wider comms team and channels, which meets every month. It's not entirely joined up, but it's a start!'

The increasing importance of digital
We mentioned above that your aim is to get your story in front of the people who should be reading it, on the devices or channels through which they access their information. Today, it's all about digital.

Who is the audience?
Most companies know who they want their audiences to be – a combination in varying degrees of the stakeholder groups discussed in Chapter 1. But working out how to address them via digital channels is far more difficult than it is via the medium of the annual report, because of the pervasiveness of digital in all aspects of life today, and the inability to control how people navigate information online. Digital, particularly social media (more on that below), offers a direct, two-way relationship with individuals, so when you're thinking about communicating online, it's essential you never forget this very different dynamic. Back to the investor audience for a moment: a 2021 survey by PR firm Brunswick of 328 institutional investors across the UK, US and Canada found that 'In 2020, digital sources powered more trading decisions and investment recommendations than ever before'. Notably, the IR section of the corporate website was cited as 'the most used and trusted of all of the sources... tested', with 72% of respondents saying they made an investment decision 'based on something they learned there'. This speaks to the fundamental importance of reporting well in building trust, since it is reporting content that largely forms the basis of IR websites.

Readers or users?
Most people access annual reports online, but the long-form presentation and design of the annual report is still essentially a print form, designed for in-depth reading. From what we've observed over the years, people who want to do more than look things up in an annual report tend to print off the bits they want to read. The need for long-form narrative and explanation of complex information in a trustworthy, and therefore static, format has not changed, which is why the annual report retains its essential place.

However, almost all the other ways companies reach their audiences today are digital. At this point it may be useful to bear in mind that people read reports but they use websites. In almost two decades of working in digital corporate communications, I have rarely heard any 'user' of a website or other form of digital media described as a 'reader'. People using websites are described as users and the art of delivering content to them is called 'the user experience'. What's the point of this distinction? Put simply, the long-form content that works so beautifully for a reader of reports doesn't work for a user of websites.

This is partly because, with websites, you have even less control over how people navigate the information than you do with a PDF form or printed report. At least with a PDF, the order of the pages and sections is fixed, and it's obvious that you mean people to start on page 1, even if they don't. With a website, you can give an indication of importance through the top-level navigation running left to right (most important things on the left, unless you have an alphabet reading from the right), and the sub-navigation running top to bottom.

However, if people arrive via Google, then they land on the page best related to their search term, which may not be where you intended them to start. And when they get there, they will then only engage with your story if it's presented appropriately for the medium – and the digital channel opens up a vast array of possibilities to capture people's imagination. Film, animation, graphics; as well as words and pictures. Just think about your own experience online and what does and doesn't engage you.

You have about three seconds to grab your audience

Let's assume that your user has landed on a page you want them to go to. Now it's a matter of holding their attention. Anecdotal evidence suggests that the average time a person spends on a webpage before moving on is about three seconds, if nothing grabs their attention. So you have a very, very small window of opportunity.

This is where clarity of message, engaging language, great visuals and every other communications tool you can think of come into play. And, you need to make sure that whatever content you create will work well on *all* the devices people may be accessing it from. Most people will be looking at things on the go on their smartphones (and network access can be patchy so download speeds matter); some may be on iPads or similar; but only if you're lucky will your user be sitting at a desk with a nice big screen and a brilliant download speed.

The vital importance of social media
Getting information online used to be just about looking things up – the original worldwide web was basically a giant encyclopaedia. But today, the digital world is driven largely by social media. So far so obvious; however corporate communication in general hasn't fully caught up with this phenomenon.

Whatever its drawbacks, social media is touching every aspect of life, and corporate life is no exception. But, even though most FTSE companies now use Twitter to communicate with investors and other stakeholders, aside from a small handful of tech companies, I'd argue that most of UK or even global plc are chasing their social media reputation, not leading it. For good or ill, social media is even beginning to influence investment decisions, particularly of the younger generation, with one in five institutional investors under 30 using Reddit to make an investment decision, even though the platform is not itself highly trusted. And, overall, as the Brunswick survey found, a 'more digitally-reliant investment community made online sources and social media even more central to information sharing and decision-making', with social media channels YouTube and LinkedIn increasing in importance by 18% and 12% respectively over the past year.

Make or break your reputation
For social media reputation, read reputation in general. Regulators are no longer the arbiters of corporate reputation – and the extent to which they ever were is debatable, given the corporate scandals that have occurred despite regulatory intervention (see the crisis cycle in Chapter 1).

Studies show that consumers are more likely to trust organisations that are active on social media. In 2018, Edelman's Trust Barometer did a special report on brands and social media, which found that 'four in 10 consumers say they are unlikely to become emotionally attached to a brand unless they are interacting via social media'. Also, 59% were 'more likely to believe a direct communication than advertising', although there was also a high degree of concern over the misuse of social media, with the report noting that brands 'must act to address data privacy concerns, create trusted content, and join forces with regulators, platforms and consumers to restore trust in the social media ecosystem'.

The importance of social media in building trust makes sense: active use of social media implies that a company is interested in a two-way dialogue. It's true that it can also expose you to a higher degree of risk because of greater transparency, but today, where there is nowhere to hide, the risk of silence – and someone else filling the vacuum for you – is even greater. But what you say has to be true – or you'll get found out. A 2019 survey of business owners carried out by Brother UK and Telegraph Spark found that social media is the main technology that 35% of business owners would be focusing on over the next 12 months. The article also made the point that what businesses do with social media has to be real – 'social media can be used to build public trust in your business, but only if your business and the people who run it are actually trustworthy'.

> **Social media is touching every aspect of life, and corporate life is no exception – and studies show that consumers are more likely to trust organisations that are active on social media.**

Through social media, consumers and other corporate stakeholders are increasingly holding companies to account – think oil spills, or air pollution. But, with the tendency of bad news to go viral, someone doesn't need to be a direct stakeholder at all to trash a corporate reputation these days. Sadly, it's a lot harder to make good news go viral than bad, human nature being what it is, but that's all the more reason why you must have open, honest, consistent and believable communications. How credible can your message be if it's not where your audience expects to find it? Or in a format they expect to receive it?

This is why companies need to join it all up and think hard about how they are going to use the channels used by their audiences to control their own story – or at least make their version of it the one that people believe.

Be true to your message, whatever the channel
To come back to the annual report, using that story you've created as the foundation of your communications doesn't of course mean that other things won't be communicated throughout the year. But the story about your business contained in the annual report is the intellectual basis – the brief, if you like – for how you should deal with and communicate about everything else that happens.

For example, if you're a manufacturing firm, in your annual report you're probably going to talk about the high environmental standards you have in your plants, and the care you take to have open and honest communications with local stakeholders. So, when your processing plant in rural Brazil, say, develops a fault and accidentally tips a load of chemicals into a local river, fouling the watercourse and killing wildlife, what are you going to say – and do – about it? If your annual report is telling the truth, then you won't wait for days or weeks until the lawyers allow you to put out a bland statement. Instead you'll get online quickly, take responsibility, explain what happened and why, how you're containing it, and how you're going to redeem the situation, and improve your systems to make sure it doesn't happen again.

Coming back to the social media point, if you don't do that, if you don't own the story quickly, you can be sure someone else will spread the word online, and you'll have a much bigger mess to sort out than if you'd been honest – and speedily so – in the first place.

People expect bad corporate behaviour. Surprise them, behave well, and they'll start to believe what you say.

And just think – in responding well, and managing your communications consistently throughout the year, you'll have some great case studies and examples to back up what you say about yourselves when it comes to next year's annual report. ■

A!

To recap
- The essence of trust is consistency – so make sure you're consistent in everything you say and do
- Your company story has to be defined in the annual report – so use it to help you achieve consistency everywhere through a coherent comms plan, and in the process get a better return on your annual report investment
- Everyone's online – make sure you are too, in the places your stakeholders expect to find you, in formats that will engage and inspire them
- Use social media to create an honest, direct relationship with individual stakeholders
- Don't hide – you'll get found out, and forever be trying to repair the damage
- Tell the truth – it's the right and sensible thing to do, and your stakeholders will thank you for it.

Useful sources

REGULATIONS AND CODES

The Companies Act 2006

- 2018 Amendments to the Companies Act: The Companies (Miscellaneous Reporting) Regulations 2018:
www.legislation.gov.uk/ukdsi/2018/9780111170298/part/2
- 2013 Amendments to the Companies Act: The Companies Act 2006 (Strategic Report and Directors' Report) Regulations 2013:
www.legislation.gov.uk/ukdsi/2013/9780111540169/contents

Financial Conduct Authority (FCA) Handbook:
www.handbook.fca.org.uk/

Prudential Regulation Authority (PRA) Rulebook:
www.prarulebook.co.uk/

The UK Stewardship Code 2020:
www.frc.org.uk/getattachment/5aae591d-d9d3-4cf4-814a-d14e156a1d87/Stewardship-Code_Dec-19-Final-Corrected.pdf

The UK Corporate Governance Code 2018:
www.frc.org.uk/getattachment/88bd8c45-50ea-4841-95b0-d2f4f48069a2/2018-UK-Corporate-Governance-Code-FINAL.pdf

The Wates Corporate Governance Principles for Large Private Companies (2018):
www.frc.org.uk/getattachment/31dfb844-6d4b-4093-9bfe-19cee2c29cda/Wates-Corporate-Governance-Principles-for-LPC-Dec-2018.pdf

The EU Transparency Directive (2004, revised 2013):
www.esma.europa.eu/regulation/corporate-disclosure/transparency-directive

London Stock Exchange: Corporate Governance for Main Market and AIM Companies (2012):
www.londonstockexchange.com/companies-and-advisors/aim/publications/documents/corpgov.pdf

GOVERNMENT-COMMISSIONED REVIEWS

The Brydon Review – Assess, Assure and Inform: Improving Audit Quality and Effectiveness, Report of the Independent Review into the Quality and Effectiveness of Audit (2019):
assets.publishing.service.gov.uk/government/uploads/system/uploads/attachment_data/file/852960/brydon-review-final-report.pdf

The CMA Review – Competition and Markets Authority Statutory Audit Services Market Study (2019):
assets.publishing.service.gov.uk/media/5d03667d40f0b609ad3158c3/audit_final_report_02.pdf

The Kingman Review – Independent Review of the Financial Reporting Council (2018):
assets.publishing.service.gov.uk/government/uploads/system/uploads/attachment_data/file/767387/frc-independent-review-final-report.pdf

Corporate Governance Reform: the Government Response to the Green Paper Consultation (2017):
assets.publishing.service.gov.uk/government/uploads/system/uploads/attachment_data/file/640470/corporate-governance-reform-government-response.pdf

The Kay Review of UK Equity Markets and Long-term Decision Making (2012):
assets.publishing.service.gov.uk/government/uploads/system/uploads/attachment_data/file/253454/bis-12-917-kay-review-of-equity-markets-final-report.pdf

The Walker Review – A Review of Corporate Governance in UK Banks and other Financial Industry Entities (2009):
webarchive.nationalarchives.gov.uk/+/
www.hm-treasury.gov.uk/d/walker_review_261109.pdf

The Cadbury Report – Review of the (Corporate Governance) Committee on the Financial Aspects of Corporate Governance (1992):
www.icaew.com/-/media/corporate/files/library/subjects/corporate-governance/financial-aspects-of-corporate-governance.ashx?la=en

The Government Response to the Green Paper Consultation on Corporate Governance Reform (August 2017):
assets.publishing.service.gov.uk/government/uploads/system/uploads/attachment_data/file/640470/corporate-governance-reform-government-response.pdf

SUSTAINABILITY/ESG-RELATED SOURCES

The Task Force on Climate-Related Financial Disclosures:
www.fsb-tcfd.org/

Climate Disclosure Standards Board:
www.cdsb.net/

Global Reporting Initiative:
www.globalreporting.org/

SASB Standards from the Value Reporting Foundation:
www.sasb.org/

The Value Reporting Foundation:
www.valuereportingfoundation.org

REVIEWS OF REPORTING

Black Sun, Horizon Series – The Ecosystem of Authenticity, Analysis of FTSE 100 Corporate Reporting Trends in 2019:
www.blacksunplc.com/horizon

Radley Yeldar, The Battle for Annual Reporting (2019):
www.ry.com/our-thinking/the-battle-for-annual-reporting/

PwC's Annual Review of Corporate Reporting in the FTSE 350:
www.pwc.co.uk/services/audit/insights/ftse-350-reporting-trends.html

Grant Thornton's Annual Corporate Governance Review:
www.grantthornton.co.uk/insights/corporate-governance-review-2020/

OTHER USEFUL SOURCES

#WTFW?! – the Falcon Windsor monthly blog:
www.falconwindsor.com/blog

The Chartered Governance Institute:
www.cgi.org.uk

EY's Corporate Governance and Reporting Insights:
www.ey.com/en_uk/assurance/corporate-governance-and-reporting

Addleshaw Goddard produces regular updates and runs seminars focused on governance and compliance issues, particularly annual reporting. Their Governance & Compliance Portal aggregates all sources of law, regulation and guidance related to reporting, among other issues.
www.addleshawgoddard.com/en/specialisms/corporate/governance-and-compliance/

FRC Guidance on Reports and Reporting from the FRC Reporting Lab:
www.frc.org.uk/investors/financial-reporting-lab

FRC Future of Corporate Reporting Project:
www.frc.org.uk/accountants/accounting-and-reporting-policy/clear-and-concise-and-wider-corporate-reporting/frc-future-of-corporate-reporting-project

Institute of Chartered Accountants in England and Wales:
www.icaew.com/

Legal & General Investment Management Insights:
www.lgim.com/uk/en/insights/

PwC Corporate Reporting Insights:
www.pwc.co.uk/services/audit/corporate-reporting.html

BOOKS ON HOW TO WRITE WELL

John Simmons
- *We, Me, Them and It: The Power of Words in Business*, Texere, 2000
- *The Invisible Grail: In Search of the True Language of Brands*, Texere, 2003
- *Dark Angels: How Writing Releases Creativity at Work*, Cyan, 2004

The Dark Angels Collective
- *On Writing,* Unbound, 2019

Acronyms and abbreviations

AGM	annual general meeting
AIM	Alternative Investment Market
ARGA	Audit, Reporting and Governance Authority
CEO	chief executive officer
CFO	chief financial officer
CMS	content management system
CSDB	Climate Standards Disclosure Board
EPIC	Embankment Project for Inclusive Capitalism
ESEF	European Single Electronic Format
ESG	environmental, social and governance
ESMA	European Securities and Markets Authority
FBU	fair, balanced and understandable
FCA	Financial Conduct Authority
FRC	Financial Reporting Council
GRI	Global Reporting Initiative
IA	The Investment Association
IFRS	International Financial Reporting Standards
IIRC	International Integrated Reporting Council
KPI	key performance indicator
NGO	non-governmental organisation
QCA	Quoted Companies Alliance
REIT	real estate investment trust
SASB	Sustainability Accounting Standards Board
SRI	socially responsible investment
TCFD	Task Force on Climate-related Financial Disclosures
UNGC	United Nations Global Compact
UN SDGs	United Nations Sustainable Development Goals
VRF	Value Reporting Foundation (formed from the merger of the IIRC and SASB in 2021)

Acknowledgements

My first thank you has to be a combined one to Dark Angels and The Chartered Governance Institute. I'm really grateful to the Institute for commissioning me to write this book, and it's thanks to Dark Angels that they did. The team from the Institute saw my blog about the corporate reporting chapter I'd written in *On Writing*, Dark Angels' book on how to write well for business, published in June 2019. And, in a happy circularity, the reason The Chartered Governance Institute was on my blog mailing list in the first place was through their business development director, Charis Evans, whom I met through her sister Verity, who was on the first Dark Angels course I did in early 2007. So I'd like to thank Charis and the others from The Chartered Governance Institute – Maria Brookes, Kristen Harding, Sheida Heidari (former editor), Saqib Lal Saleem, Manon Lefebvre, Ben O'Hagan, Kate Ray and Peter Swabey.

What is Dark Angels? In simple terms it's a group of associate partners (I'm one) who run creative writing for business courses, based on the philosophy that business writing should be more human. But once a Dark Angel, always a Dark Angel, and so it's become a network of amazing writers who are promoting the cause of good writing throughout the business world, and who are also lovely human beings. In the challenging times we've all faced this year, Dark Angels has been a godsend to many, keeping people connected and supported through inspiring words.

I therefore want to thank my Dark Angels associate partners, John Simmons, Jamie Jauncey, Neil Baker, Richard Pelletier, Gillian Colhoun, Mike Gogan, Martin Lee, Elen Lewis, Andy Milligan, Craig Watson and Stuart Delves. Particularly John Simmons who, throughout his long and distinguished career, has been an inspiration to many a writer and designer. And, I want to thank my Dark Angels cohort for being supportive writing colleagues, as well as wonderful friends:

Heather Atchison (who was also a contributor to this book), Chris Davenport, Janet Gordon, Thomas Heath, Jonathan Holt, Gordon Kerr, Jo Macsween, Paul Redstone and Anelia Varela.

I also remember with gratitude the late Neil Duffy, one of my Dark Angels cohort, who advised me in business, supported me in life, and was constant to the end, which came far too soon in 2017.

And so to my fellow writers – Heather I've already mentioned, but I'd like to thank her again, along with Adrian, Kerry, Neil, Mark and Jay for joining me in writing this book, which is so much better as a collective book than it would ever have been if I'd tried to write it on my own. It's also much better because it's been so beautifully designed, and for that I need to thank Mark Noad, Peter Copley and Justine Miller, the brilliant design team at Falcon Windsor. Writing a book during corporate reporting season would have been impossible without the support of the rest of the FW team as well, who, by pulling together, enabled me to take the time off I needed – Sophie Chisholm, Richard Hammerton (to whom I'm also eternally grateful for proof reading this book), Paul Keilthy, Tamara O'Brien, Fiona Smith, Sam Webb and Alison Woolven.

I also want to thank those who agreed to be featured in the book which has made it a far richer source of ideas and inspiration – Martin Ansley-Young, Will Chalk, Andy Griffiths, Maria Kepa, Paul Lee, Ben Mathews, Rachael Matzopoulos, Andrew Ninian, Richard Preston, Sacha Sadan, Thomas Toomse-Smith and Robert Riche. And, I'd like to thank Sir Donald Brydon for his excellent foreword, as well as his wise words on 'best practice'.

As you can imagine, I had many readers who offered the very best of constructive criticism, and gave me their time, also during reporting season. A huge thanks therefore to Gill Hodge, Nicola Foster, Harriet Howey, Annie Heaton, Karen Almeida, Simon Harper, Lorraine Clover, Roger Evans, Robert Eccles. And, to my agency colleagues who gave their pearls of wisdom for Chapter 5: Karen Almeida, Clive Bidwell, Sallie Pilot, Dean Radley and Miles Wratten.

I also want to thank Polly Garland, who did the heavy lifting on data for the second edition, along with the many people who were kind enough to talk to me during my research for this book, or otherwise were supportive sounding boards, including Steve Allen, Martin Blaxall, Ian Brownhill, Alex Burr, Alissa Clarke, Pamela Coles, Miranda Craig, David Croft, Danielle Cyrus, Karen Donhue, Sally Fairbairn, Andrew Fairhurst, Russell Gammon, Ewa Gebala, Kate Gill, Liz Grahame, Michael Hirschl, Alan Knight, Janice Lingwood, Iain MacLeod, Chris Marsh, Annie Mickle, Desna Martin, Peter Mason, Claire Moynihan, Claire-Marie O'Grady, Archi Quddus, Deepa Raval, Arthur Reeves, Jessica Rouleau, Shona Sabnis, Anna Swaithes, Anna Taylor, Jaime Tham, Penny Thomas, Robert Welch, Ben Wielgus. Plus all those others who'd prefer not to be mentioned by name!

But I must mention by name with gratitude the others who've listened endlessly to me going on about the book through its various iterations – my husband David Bodanis who has magnanimously supported another author in the house, and my son Julius Falcon who forgives much, as do Anna Rowlands, Roger and Maxine Windsor, Guy and Michaela Windsor, Richard and Nadine Windsor, Rebecca Windsor and Isabel Windsor.

Finally – this book could not have been written without the experience I've gained over the nearly 20 years I've worked in corporate reporting. My very first reporting client was Tate & Lyle, and it's thanks to Rowan Adams and Chris Fox that it turned out to be such an inspiring and rewarding experience – and still is today, which remains thanks to Rowan, to whom this book is dedicated and to whom I owe a huge debt of gratitude. Besides Tate & Lyle, I'm also forever grateful to all Falcon Windsor's clients, who've given us inspiring and interesting work over the years as well as supporting us in many other ways too, and to the wider Falcon Windsor network of colleagues and friends who are so fundamental to the flourishing of a small company like ours.

Contributors' biographies

Mark Forsyth – *Prologue*
Mark is the author of three books on the English language: *The Etymologicon* which was a *Sunday Times* No. 1 bestseller, *The Horologicon* and *The Elements of Eloquence*. He has also written *The Unknown Unknown* on the joy of bookshops, *Christmas Cornucopia* on the origins of festive traditions, and *A Short History of Drunkenness*. Mark's books have been translated into more than 15 languages.

Adrian Hornsby – *Chapter 1*
Adrian is an award-winning writer across a diverse portfolio of forms and interests, ranging from reporting and impact assessment to international development, urbanism and hi-tech music theatre. His books include *The Good Analyst* ('the Bible of social impact', COO, Big Society Capital) and *The Chinese Dream* ('an absorbing encyclopaedic monster of a book', *Icon*); theatre includes *As Big As The Sky* (with Ai Weiwei, 'an opera of striking invention', *The Wire*). His groundbreaking opera for binaural headphones, *The Hearing*, is due to premiere at the Holland Festival in 2021. Adrian works with Falcon Windsor on corporate reporting and other writing projects.

Kerry Watson – *Chapter 3*
Kerry has nearly 20 years' experience in the corporate governance field having worked as Company Secretary for FTSE companies in the engineering and energy sectors. As well as being heavily involved in corporate transactions including acquisitions and takeovers, Kerry is experienced in building and refining governance processes, and drafting as well as producing company annual reports in line with UK compliance and governance requirements. Kerry is a member of The Chartered Governance Institute.

Heather Atchison – *Chapter 4*

Heather has spent the best part of 20 years helping organisations of all types hone their brand language, so that they reflect their culture and personality both in what they say about themselves and in how they say it. As creative director at two UK communications agencies and then as an independent strategist, trainer and writer, she's created and rolled out brand voices for many well-known companies and organisations. She believes that all company messaging should be engaging and on-brand, wherever it may be – corporate communications included. To that end, Heather has helped many Falcon Windsor clients tell their stories.

Neil Roberts – *Chapter 6*

Neil began his communications career in 2000 when he joined the founding team at Investis, developing what was then a new digital approach to investor communications. He was a key member of the senior management team that took Investis from niche, IR-focused start-up to international digital agency, working with many UK and European plcs in many different sectors along the way. Neil joined Falcon Windsor in 2019 as the company's first managing director.

Jay Sheth – *Company case studies*

Jay was formerly Head of Economics, Policy and Regulatory Affairs at Virgin Money. Whilst at Virgin Money, he co-led the company's work on the HM Treasury Women in Finance (WIF) Review and subsequent HMT WIF Charter. Jay left Virgin Money in late 2019 to spend some time travelling around Central Asia, indulging his great interest in the countries of the former Soviet Union. Before Virgin Money, he worked for the European Commission, the CBI and the Treasury Committee, and in the UK Houses of Parliament as a Senior Economist and Policy Specialist. This included a secondment to the Parliamentary Commission on Banking Standards (PCBS), where he was part of the team that drafted the final report of the Commission on culture and standards in banking. Jay is a trustee of the Hackney Empire and a member of the advisory board of Women in Banking and Finance (WIBF).

Chapter notes

NOTES TO CHAPTER 1

1. Mackay, Charles, *Extraordinary Popular Delusions and the Madness of Crowds* (1841, ed. Litrix Reading Room, 2001), p.39.
2. Harris, Ron, 'The Bubble Act: Its Passage and Its Effects on Business Organization', *The Journal of Economic History*, Vol. 54, No. 3, 1994, p.610. After the Bubble Act, share issuing and holding continued for companies that either had a Royal Charter or had been granted a special Act of Parliament. This effectively restricted shares to large companies with influential directors. Small companies went back to raising modest amounts of capital from family, friends and banks.
3. Average annual report page length of the FTSE 350; PwC, *PwC's Annual Review of Corporate Reporting in the FTSE 350 2019/20* (2020).
4. Edwards, John Richard, *A History of Corporate Financial Reporting in Britain* (Routledge, 2019), p.8.
5. This figure draws on Edwards' Figure 1.2, ibid. p.8.
6. PwC, *Global investor survey on corporate reporting* (November 2017), p.4. The statement put to investors in full was: 'I have enough trust in the information companies report on strategic goals, risks and key performance indicators for me to be confident in my analysis and decision making.'
7. 2021 Edelman Trust Barometer, Global Report, p.42.
8. From Greta Thunberg's speech at the UN Climate Change Conference COP25, 11 December 2019.
9. FRC, *Annual Review of Corporate Reporting 2015/16* (2016), p.12.
10. Ibid.
11. Brydon, Donald, *Assess, Assure and Inform: Improving Audit Quality and Effectiveness* (Crown Review, 2019), p.4. See case study on the Brydon Review on pp. 94-97 of this book.
12. Change in the number of FTSE 350 companies making some disclosure on stakeholder engagement from 2017/18 to 2018/19. PwC, *PwC's Annual Review of Corporate Reporting in the FTSE 350 2018/19* (2019), p.9.
13. FRC, *Guidance on the Strategic Report* (2018), p.57. Section 172 itself was introduced in the Companies Act 2006, and has therefore been around for some time. What is new is the need to make a specific statement about it.
14. Appears five times in the FRC's *Guidance on the Strategic Report* (2018): pp.3, 5, 13, 23, 89.
15. Radley Yeldar, *The Battle For Annual Reporting* (2019), p.18.
16. PwC, *PwC's Annual Review of Corporate Reporting in the FTSE 350 2018/19* (2019), p.18.

NOTES TO CHAPTER 2

1. *Financial Times*, 26 April 2021,
   www.ft.com/content/262f2dfa-82bc-4454-96aa-bc5c38f82cdd
2. Black Sun, Horizon Series: *The Ecosystem of Authenticity, Analysis of FTSE 100 Corporate Reporting Trends in 2019*, p.42.
3. Robert Eccles: The Purpose Of The IBC/WEF Stakeholder Capitalism Metrics Initiative: A Conversation With Brian Moynihan, *Forbes*, 19 December, 2020.
4. Ibid

NOTES TO CHAPTER 3

1. Deloitte: *Annual report insights 2020, Surveying FTSE reporting.*

NOTES TO SPOTLIGHT ON SMALL-CAP COMPANIES

1. FRC/ICAEW: Smaller Listed and AIM Quoted Companies, A Practical Guide for Audit Committees on Improving Financial Reporting (2015), p4.
2. FRC: Corporate Reporting Thematic Review, Reporting by Smaller Listed and AIM Quoted Companies (2018), p6.

NOTES TO CHAPTER 6

1. Edelman Trust Barometer 2021,
   www.edelman.com/trustbarometer
2. Brunswick Digital Investor Survey, March 2021,
   www.brunswickgroup.com/digital-investor-survey-2021-i18508/
3. Ibid.
4. Edelman Trust Barometer Special Report: Brand and Social Media,
   www.edelman.co.uk/research/edelman-trust-barometer-special-report-brand-and-social-media
5. *The Telegraph*, 8 October, 2019,
   www.telegraph.co.uk/business/ready-and-enabled/building-brand-trust-through-social-media/

Index

Abbreviations 242
Acronyms 242
Agency (reporting) 191-211
  budgeting 204-207
  creative process 198-199
  definition of an agency 195
  finding the right agency 118
  principles of a good client/agency
    partnership 195-197
  tendering and pitching 207-210
  The Vitec Group plc, why we use an
    agency 186
  working well with an agency, Chapter 5,
    191-211
Annual report *passim*
Approval process 131-133
  Audit Committee 131-132
  auditor 133
  directors/Board 132
  final sign-off 132-133
Audit, Reporting and Governance Authority
  (ARGA) *see also Financial Reporting
  Council (FRC)*
  creation of 21
Auditors *see also approval process*
  future of audit (the Brydon Review)
    100-103
  perspectives on reporting from an
    auditor (interview) 109-112
  regulation and the role of the auditor 26
  working with your auditor 128

Best practice, advice against 6-7
Board *passim*
Briefing (design, editorial, strategic) *passim*
  elements of a good brief 169-172
  process 198-200
  relationship to wider communications
    228-231
  why you need one 167-168, 206
Brydon Review, the (Assess, Assure and
  Inform: Improving Audit Quality and
  Effectiveness, Report of the Independent
  Review into the Quality and Effectiveness
  of Audit, 2019) 100-103

Budgeting 204-207
  return on your investment in the
    annual report 226
Business model
  as part of the corporate story 45
  importance of (auditor's view) 109

Committees
  Board committees, process and
    approvals 124, 132-123
  importance of Board Committee
    chairmen's letters (lawyer's view) 62
  writing and editing by committee 165
Communication *passim*
  general communications planning and
    relationship with annual report
    229-231
  importance of annual report to wider
    communications channels 129-130
Companies' Act 2006 21
  link to download 238
  section 172 35, 36
Compliance *passim*
  compliance versus communication
    (lawyer's view) 60-62
  'cut the clutter' 121-122
  US regulatory system 151
Contributors
  Ansley-Young, Martin, Arup 155-157
  Chalk, Will, Addleshaw Goddard 59-63
  Griffiths, Andy, The Investor Forum
    213-215
  Kepa, Maria, EY 109-112
  Lee, Paul, the Brydon Review 100-103
  Mathews, Ben, BP plc 151-153
  Matzopoulos, Rachael, The Vitec
    Group plc 183-186
  Ninian, Andrew, The Investment
    Association 213-215
  Preston, Richard, Addleshaw Goddard
    59-63
  Riche, Robert, Friend Studio 92-95
  Toomse-Smith, Thomas, Financial
    Reporting Council 96-99
  Sadan, Sacha, Legal & General
    Investment Management 105-107
Copywriting *see writing*

Index

Corporate governance *passim*
   changes for large private companies 158-159
   differences for small-cap companies 187
   writing the corporate governance report 52-53
Corporate Governance Code (UK) 21
   'fair, balanced and understandable' 131-132
Climate Standards Disclosure Board (CSDB) 34

Dark Angels creative writing for business group and courses 243-244
Design *passim, see also agency*
   of this book 8
   importance of, and how to do it well 161-181
Digital *see also ESEF, website*
   ESEF (European Single Electronic Format) production 134
   how digital is shaping communication 232-235
   using digital channels for reporting, FRC Future of Corporate Reporting Project 96
Directors *passim, see also approvals process*
   remuneration report 52-54
   role of in reporting 24-31
   managing directors' involvement in the annual report 122-123
Disclosure, *passim, see also regulation*
   'cut the clutter' 121-122
   non-financial reporting frameworks 71-75
   history of and increasing requirements for 22-37
   lawyer's view 59-63
   required disclosure outside the annual report 71-73
Drafting *see also editing*
   company story 39-51
   how to write 161-177
   process and managing inputs 121-122, 126-127
Dual-listed companies, case study 151-154

Editing/editor *passim*
   editing by committee 165
   editorial board 126
   editorial calendar (general communications) 230
   editorial guidelines (general communications) 230
   editorial read (out loud) 139
   process 199
   single editorial voice 168-172; The Vitec Group plc, value of a single editor, 185
   technology (editing PDFs etc) 129, 136-137
Environmental, social and governance (ESG) issues *passim*
   investor interest 76-81
   investor's view (Andy Griffiths, The Investor Forum) 215
   non-financial reporting frameworks 74-75
European Single Electronic Format (ESEF)
   discussion of its development; lack of usefulness 86-91
   how to manage the ESEF 134
European Securities and Markets Authority (ESMA) *in relation to ESEF* 86-89

Fair, balanced and understandable (FBU) 24-25, 70
   ensuring your report is FBU 131-132
   including the FBU requirement in your brief 170
Financial Reporting Council (FRC) *see also ARGA*
   2015 review: Improving the Quality of Reporting by Smaller Listed and AIM Quoted Companies 188
   Future of Corporate Reporting Project 96-99
   guidance on using plain language 175
   guidance on narrative reporting 45
   replacement by ARGA 21, 31
Financial statements *passim*
   importance of good writing 181
   tagging in relation to ESEF 86-95
   why this book is not a guide to producing them 4
Form 20F 71, 151

Global Reporting Initiative (GRI) 34, 74
Governance *passim*
　writing the governance report 52-53

International Financial Reporting
　Standards (IFRS) 4, 97, 187
International Integrated Reporting Council
　(IIRC) 71, 74
Investors *passim*
　increasing interest in ESG reporting
　　76-81, 215
　types of investor or shareholder 213
　views 11-13, 97-99, 213-215, 217-219

Key performance indicators (KPIs) 29,
　31, 44-45 *see also story*
　how to make KPIs part of your story
　　50-51
　relationship with remuneration 53

Large private companies, case study 155-159

Marketplace (business environment),
　reporting on 45
Materiality (i.e. relevance) 70
　an exercise in connecting the flow
　– context and materiality 49-50
　determining what is material 69-73

Narrative reporting *passim*
　ESEF and narrative reporting 84-88
　FRC guidance 45
　how to write your story 39-56
Non-financial reporting frameworks 71-75
Non-statutory reporting 67-81, 83

Online *passim, see also digital,*
　production, website
Out-loud read 139

Photography
　as part of design 178
　planning and briefing 127, 171, 199
Project management
　approvals and sign-off *see approvals*
　budgeting 204-207
　checking 130

communication 128-129
creating a team 124-126
involving different business units
　or divisions 126
linking up with other year-end processes
　129-130
managing feedback 125-131
managing internal stakeholders 122-123
photography *see photography*
planning and preparation 118-127
production *see production, online;*
　production, print
proof reading *see proof reading*
remote working *see remote working*
responsibilities of the project team
　125-126
timetable 124
working with an agency 118, 191-211
Production, online *see also digital, website*
　ESEF 128 *see also European Single*
　Electronic Format (ESEF)
　publishing the annual report online
　　133, 179-180
Production, print and distribution
　134, 146-148
　book proof 147
　checking final proofs 148
　choosing paper 146
　planning 146
　scatter proofs 147, 148
Proof reading 132-133 199
Proofs *passim*
Purpose *see also Financial Reporting*
　Council, Future of Corporate
　Reporting Project
　of a company, and reporting on it
　　36-37, 43, 45, 53
　of the annual report *passim*
　evolution of the purpose of the
　　annual report 67-69, 103

Regulation, regulator *passim, see also*
　disclosure, ESEF, reporting
　developments and future of 67-83
　dual listing 152
　FRC Future of Corporate Reporting
　　Project 96-99

history and increasing burden of 18-27
lawyer's view 59-63
useful sources 238
why this book doesn't describe the regulations 17
why regulators should work with practitioners 82
Remote working, challenges of 135-142
added costs 143
creative/ideas process 143-144
editorial and proof reading 139
keeping focused 142
managing people and comments 140-141
technology and equipment 136-137
version control and file storage 137-138
Remuneration *passim, see also directors*
remuneration report 52-54
Reporting *passim*
history and evolution of 18-27
where reporting is going and why 67-83
Risk reporting *passim*
as part of the company story 39-51
investor's view 106
reporting on climate risk 74 *see also TCFD*
knowing your risks and reporting well 71-72

Section 172 of Companies Act 2006 35, 55, 68
large private companies 159
Shareholders *see investors*
Small cap companies, case study 183-188
Social media *see also digital* 234-235
Stakeholders *passim, see also section 172*
who they are as readers of your report 32-37
interests 67-69
Strategic report *passim*
how to write the strategic report 39-56, 163-177
Strategy *passim*
Story *passim, see also editorial, writing*
context and materiality 49-50
FRC contents list 45
how to write a story 39-56, 163-177
importance of flow 44

KPIs and performance 50-51
language 173-177
strategy and action 49
what is a story? 40-42
Sustainability Accounting Standards Board (SASB) 75
a useful approach to standardising non-financial disclosure 80-81

Task Force on Climate-related Financial Disclosures (TCFD) 34, 74
Typesetting *see also agency*
budget and costs 204-206
process 199

United Nations Global Compact (UNGC) 75
United Nations Sustainable Development Goals (UN SDGs) 75
inclusion in annual report 78
Useful sources 238-241

Website *passim, see also digital, project management, production*
publishing the annual report online 133-134, 179-180
updating your website with annual report information 133
using the annual report story as the foundation for communications 223-237
World Economic Forum International Business Council 68, 79
Writing *passim, see also editing, story*
language basics 174-177
tone of voice 170, 218
style guide 173

WEBINAR

Practical perspectives on reporting webinar series

QUARTERLY WEBINARS ON HOT TOPICS FOR REPORTING PRACTITIONERS

On the first Thursday of each quarter (January/April/July/October), 12.30-1.15pm UK time, Claire hosts a lively discussion and Q&A over Zoom on key questions for reporting. We're hearing from knowledgeable and interesting people from across the reporting spectrum – Board directors, company secretaries, auditors, regulators, lawyers, investors, influencers – and more.

Panellists during the 2020-21 monthly season included Miranda Craig, Director of Strategy and Change at the Financial Reporting Council; Ben Mathews, Company Secretary of BP; Veronica Poole, Vice Chair of Deloitte UK; Professor Robert Eccles, Founding Chairman of SASB; Andy Griffiths, Executive Director of the UK's Investor Forum; Jeremy Osborn of the Value Reporting Foundation; Nadine Windsor, Global Head of Credit Trading at First Abu Dhabi Bank; governance expert Chris Hodge; and many more.

Sign up and join the debate!

For booking and links to watch past webinars

trustmeimlisted.com/webinars

> 66 *The three of you spoke with genuine feeling and insightfulness. Far too many webinars do not rise beyond blandishments, but I certainly couldn't accuse you of your colleagues of that. For that, you have my sincere thanks.* 99
> Governance professional, UK

TRAINING

Respect your reader: skills for writing an effective annual report

GET A HEAD START ON REPORT WRITING WITH THE TMIL WRITING COURSE FROM FALCON WINDSOR

Since we published TMIL, a number of people have asked us about training. And so we developed a writing training workshop, consisting of two consecutive half-day sessions, based on the principles set out in the book:

Session 1: Setting yourself up to write a good report

Session 2: Powerhouse writing techniques for reporters

Running over Zoom and with a maximum of eight delegates, this interactive workshop is designed for anyone responsible for writing or reviewing strategic, governance or sustainability/ESG reports. Your trainers are Heather Atchison, writer and author of Chapter 4, and author Claire Bodanis.

£750+VAT per person

Dates and booking information

Find out more at

trustmeimlisted.com/training

Or contact **Neil Roberts**
neil@falconwindsor.com
+44 (0)7760 171940

> *An absolutely fantastic workshop which included loads of useful techniques that can immediately be put into action. A truly inspiring course that has made me excited for the start of the annual report season!*
>
> FTSE 100 non-financial reporting manager